The Stories Congregations Tell

The Stories Congregations Tell

Flourishing in the Face of Transition and Change

EDITED BY
JOEL THIESSEN
ARCH CHEE KEEN WONG
MARK CHAPMAN

WIPF & STOCK · Eugene, Oregon

THE STORIES CONGREGATIONS TELL
Flourishing in the Face of Transition and Change

Copyright © 2024 Wipf and Stock Publishers. All rights reserved. Except for brief quotations in critical publications or reviews, no part of this book may be reproduced in any manner without prior written permission from the publisher. Write: Permissions, Wipf and Stock Publishers, 199 W. 8th Ave., Suite 3, Eugene, OR 97401.

Wipf & Stock
An Imprint of Wipf and Stock Publishers
199 W. 8th Ave., Suite 3
Eugene, OR 97401

www.wipfandstock.com

PAPERBACK ISBN: 979-8-3852-0365-9
HARDCOVER ISBN: 979-8-3852-0366-6
EBOOK ISBN: 979-8-3852-0367-3

11/26/24

Where indicated Scripture quotations are taken from the New Revised Standard Version Bible: Catholic Edition, copyright © 1989, 1993 the Division of Christian Education of the National Council of the Churches of Christ in the United States of America. Used by permission. All rights reserved.

To church and denominational leaders seeking to nurture faithful and flourishing congregations that tell meaningful stories.

Contents

	Acknowledgments	ix
1	Congregations as Storytelling Organizations *Joel Thiessen, Arch Chee Keen Wong, and Mark Chapman*	1
2	Explosively Alive: Stories of Catholic Renewal *Cathy Holtmann and Sam Reimer*	11
3	Cultivating Repertoires of Resilience: Storying Challenges and Change Towards Future Flourishing *Katie Steeves, Jason John Burtt, and Michael Wilkinson*	30
4	Flourishing in a Post-Christian Context: Two "Accessible" and "Relevant" Evangelical Churches in Quebec *Frédéric Dejean*	43
5	Stories of Spiritual Formation and Growth at St. John's Anglican Church: The Importance of Social Ties *Arch Chee Keen Wong*	63
6	Resonant Relationships: Spiritual Formation as a Congregational Focus *Mark Chapman, Andrea Chang, and James Watson*	78
7	Transitions Shaping Our Story and Identity: St. Paul's Catholic Parish *Joel Thiessen*	93

CONTENTS

8 Caring about Ascension Cares: A Profile of a Parish-Based
Community Outreach Program   108
Bernardine Ketelaars and Fr. Robert Weaver

9 Faithful Communities of Presence   122
Linda C. Nicholls, Sarah Han, and James Mallon

10 Congregations That Tell Meaningful Stories   135
Mark Chapman, Arch Chee Keen Wong, and Joel Thiessen

Index   147

Acknowledgments

OUR GRATITUDE TO THE many church leaders and congregants who graciously welcomed our research teams. Thank you for sharing your church's community and stories with us. Our collective learnings of the stories that congregations tell and the flourishing that ensues in the face of transition and change could not occur without you. We have sought to tell your stories faithfully and accurately. We hope other congregations may be positively impacted in turn.

Our editors—Joel, Arch, and Mark—want to express our appreciation for our colleagues and collaborators on this project, including many research assistants who assisted with data collection and analysis especially. We have valued your keen insights and contributions to sharpen our shared analysis of congregational life, with an eye always to the church practitioner. We are also grateful for Archbishop Linda C. Nicholls, Rev. Dr. Sarah Han, and Fr. James Mallon who carefully and thoughtfully interacted with these stories to both challenge and encourage other church leaders.

Finally, Christin Rosa—the research and program coordinator at the Flourishing Congregations Institute—provided solid administrative support to the research team, plus meticulously formatted the entire manuscript and supporting materials for publication. We are incredibly appreciative of these significant contributions.

1

Congregations as Storytelling Organizations

Joel Thiessen, Arch Chee Keen Wong, and Mark Chapman

STORIES

MOST PEOPLE LOVE A good story. Almost daily we tell and hear stories about our families, coworkers, congregations, or countries. We flock to books, Netflix, the theater, or the cinema to immerse ourselves in the stories of others. The strength of a story can depend on how a story is told, who tells the story, what content is included or excluded, the resonance between the story and the receiver's life experiences, and the connection between the storyteller and the receiver. Alter any of these elements and the story experience could change drastically.

David Boje defines a story as "an oral or written performance involving two or more people interpreting past or anticipated experience."[1] Stories just don't apply to people but to organizations as well. A storytelling organization is a "collective storytelling system in which the performance of stories is a key part of members' sense-making and a means to allow

---

1. Boje, "Stories," 1000.

them to supplement individual memories with institutional memory."[2] Applied to congregations, James Hopewell states that "narrative underlies each congregation's view of the world, its assumptions about the setting or backdrop against which its actions are sequenced, and its unique ethos thrown into visible relief."[3] Expressed differently, stories help to make and express meaning.

A guiding assumption in this book is that congregations are storytelling organizations. Most obviously, they share the Christian story to those who would listen. Less examined are the stories that congregations tell of themselves as human organizations. Think of your congregation for a moment. What storylines readily come to mind? What undergirds your church's memory and identity? Can you describe the scene, plot, actors, and props? Who are the heroes or villains? What are the high and low points? Who frames these narratives and tells your church's story? How does your church currently see itself, its surroundings, and its desired or anticipated trajectory? How have these aspects of your congregation's story evolved over time, with changes along the way in context, personnel, and so forth? How does your congregation put all these things together to make them meaningful? Questions such as these animate the storytelling organization.

In this book we—a group of social scientists and practical theologians—are interested in the stories congregations tell that, in our estimation, contribute to one or more areas of flourishing in their ministry. (We define "flourishing" later in this chapter.) We speak of "stories" rather than a single grand metanarrative "story" because different actors within the same story sometimes frame the story, perceptions, and experiences differently. Storytelling is an interactive and relational process that results in "official," public, and recorded stories and histories in the "front stage," to borrow language from sociologist Erving Goffman.[4] "Unofficial" stories in the "backstage" are also a result of these storytelling processes; unofficial stories are those that did not make the final cut but lay just beneath the surface in the minds and experiences of group members and nevertheless contribute to their understanding of the context. As Boje reminds us, "There is an official discourse and there are many marginalized discourses in every organization."[5] Part of what constitutes organizational life

---

2. Boje, "Stories," 1991.
3. Hopewell, *Congregations*, 51.
4. Goffman, *Presentation of Self*, 106–40.
5. Boje, "Stories," 1022.

is holding conflicting stories in tension with one another. This occurs by drawing upon different impression management strategies—some intentional and others unintentional—to present the organization in a particular light, however favorable or not those presentations are depending on the reference group in question.[6]

Congregations are not immune from these multilayered storytelling processes. When one talks to those in positions of power and those not in positions of power, clarity emerges on how a group sees itself, including its past, present, and potential future.[7] Depending on which stories take precedence and who decides, areas of synergy or dissonance are equally telling. The job for the social scientist is to make sense of "what is going on here," while the practical theologian not only asks what is going on here but also gives attention to what *should* be going on here.[8] In this book, an underlying thread is that where flourishing occurs, there appears to be a general synergy of storylines across a congregation (not to suggest *no* dissonance exists). That is, a group that is flourishing seems to have a shared handle on the key events, actors, scene, and plot in the life of a congregation that shapes who it is today. In broad strokes, the resultant congregational identity reflects what sociologists refer to as culture.

CONGREGATIONAL CULTURE AND IDENTITY

If we asked you to describe the DNA of your congregation, what would you say? What sets "us" apart as a church? What central traits, norms, values, beliefs, artifacts, symbols, rituals, interactions, and practices uniquely ground your church's existence, setting it apart from other churches in your tradition or down the street? How does the history of your congregation—including leaders, congregants, material and physical resources, and transitions of many kinds—influence who and what your congregation is today, and might be tomorrow?

These questions tap into a church's culture and identity—the cherished values and characteristics that demarcate one group from another and which ground the activities and associated meanings and motivations in that group. When we consider the stories that congregations tell, we

---

6. Goffman, *Presentation of Self*; Schuurman, *Subversive Evangelical*; Mulder and Marti, *Glass Church*.

7. Berger, *Invitation to Sociology*.

8. Osmer, *Practical Theology*.

are probing the cultural aspects of a church that serve as a bedrock for that church's identity. Nancy Ammerman says that "a culture includes the congregation's history and stories of its heroes. It includes its symbols, rituals, and worldview. It is shaped by the cultures in which its members live (represented by their demographic characteristics), but it takes on its own unique identity and character when those members come together."[9] Sam Reimer and Michael Wilkinson, both featured later in this book, note that "congregational cultures, like all subcultures, are emergent realities that are greater than the sum of their parts . . . because congregational cultures form not primarily from individual congregants themselves (as separate entities), but from the interaction between them."[10] Congregational culture thus encompasses the implicit and taken for granted as well as explicit norms, symbols, gestures, actions, and meanings that bind "us" together.

In addition to a congregation's own culture, they are also part of and interact with a web of other subcultures.[11] For instance, a church's denomination, theological heritage, polity structure, and ties to other religious groups and networks impact the boundary markers of what is considered normal or deviant in that local congregation. A church's physical and social location in either a rural or suburban or highly religious or secular environment also shapes the unique character of a church. So too do the sociodemographic characteristics of congregants—social class, education, occupation, ethnicity, age, and family status. Congregant traits such as these form the basis of subgroups that exist in most churches. Then there is a congregation's size, history, and leaders that shape the group's culture and identity. All these variables interact in unique ways, with changes to any variable having subtle or even substantive impacts on a congregation. For these reasons, Nancy Ammerman helpfully highlights that congregational culture is not static; it evolves as several variables interact and change over time.[12]

Congregational culture grounds a group's identity. Clarity of organizational identity is a necessary but not sufficient ingredient for congregational flourishing.[13] Our contention is that congregations must be able to identify and clearly articulate who they are and are not, and how their

9. Ammerman, "Culture and Identity," 78.
10. Reimer and Wilkinson, *Culture of Faith*, 40–41.
11. Eliasoph and Lichterman, "Culture in Interaction."
12. Ammerman, "Culture and Identity."
13. McAlpine et al., *Signs of Life*.

organizational past, present, and future link together in their context. Paying attention to the stories that congregations tell, explicitly and implicitly through their cultural artifacts, symbols, language, rituals, meanings, and interactions are helpful ways to identify a congregation's core identity—their reason for existing. In essence, this is what we do in this book, with an eye to the link between the stories that congregations tell and their own flourishing.

FLOURISHING CONGREGATIONS

Earlier research summarizes what we mean by a "flourishing congregation." Our understanding is built on an exhaustive survey of literature from around the world combined with rigorous firsthand quantitative and qualitative research in Canada.[14] Briefly, we are referring to the complex and nuanced interplay between the following domains and dimensions in congregational life: organizational ethos, including self-identity, leadership, innovation, structure, and process; internal attention, including discipleship, engaged laity, hospitable community, and diversity; and outward focus, including neighborhood involvement, partnerships, and evangelism (see fig. 1.1). These markers are intended to be broad enough to encompass the Christian theological spectrum, including Orthodox, Catholic, and mainline and conservative Protestant traditions. Theology matters here. A group's theology means that some of these traits are perceived as more salient markers of flourishing over others. For instance, evangelism may be more theologically pressing for a conservative Protestant, while proactive neighborhood involvement on a range of social justice initiatives may strike a stronger theological chord with mainline Protestants. This is not to suggest conservative Protestants have no interest in social justice endeavors or that mainline Protestants have no regard for evangelism. Our point is simply that there are certain theological and practical leanings in these distinct theological sectors.

---

14. Thiessen et al., "Flourishing Congregation"; McAlpine et al., *Signs of Life*.

Flourishing Congregations Construct

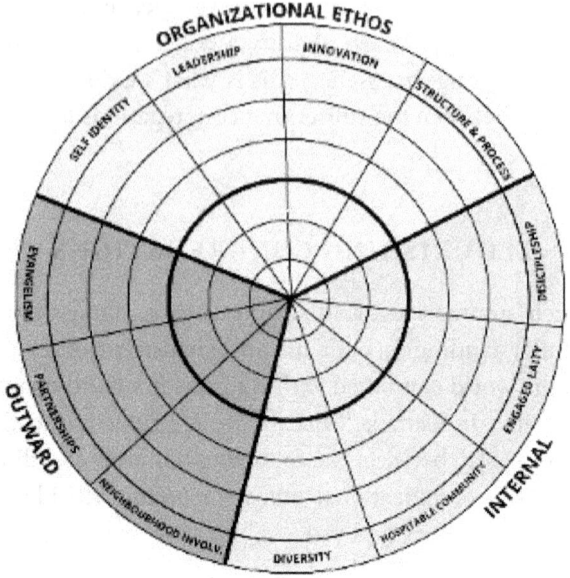

Numbers are also important to this discussion insofar as organizations need people and resources to sustain their viability. However, we do not equate numerical size or growth with flourishing, though correlations may exist at times. In the pages that follow we will hear stories from churches that range in size from less than one hundred to those in the thousands.

As will be seen throughout this book, it is also critical to stress that flourishing is a dynamic concept. Simply because a congregation is flourishing in one aspect of ministry, say discipleship or neighborhood involvement, does not mean that a congregation is flourishing in all or most other areas, such as hospitality or evangelism. Further, flourishing or floundering in an area at point *A* does not mean the same will be true at point *B*. In other words, flourishing often occurs in cycles for a myriad of reasons, as will become clear in this book. One of our central objectives is to explore the link between the stories that congregations tell and the different markers of congregational flourishing noted above.

THIS STUDY

According to Galen Watts, "Stories are not merely told, but *lived*."[15] In Boje's analysis of storytelling at Disney, he builds on a method "to observe what people actually do, rather than what they say they do."[16] Our research does both. This book captures a subset of seven case studies that were part of a larger Canada-wide project of twelve case studies involving over a dozen scholars and supported by two grants—one from the Social Sciences and Humanities Research Council of Canada and another from the Council for Christian Colleges and Universities. Two questions shaped these case studies: (1) What are the mechanisms, pathways, and processes that contribute to congregational flourishing? (2) How does congregational flourishing intersect with individuals, neighborhoods, and organizations? In our quest to interrogate these inquiries, we uncovered many other fascinating, significant, and useful lines of inquiry. This book is an attempt to tie together some of these discoveries with the two main research questions.

The following chapters detail seven Canadian-based case studies from Catholic, mainline, and conservative Protestant congregations in the Vancouver, Calgary, Toronto, London, Montreal, and Halifax regions. Congregations were selected based on reported or perceived flourishing in at least a few of the eleven dimensions of flourishing noted earlier. Some congregations were identified based on researcher knowledge of local churches in the area, and others arose from local bishop or denominational leader recommendations. Our aim was to provide as much variation as possible across the sample, including the areas of flourishing, church size, theological tradition, region, and congregant and neighborhood demographics. Each case study included a combination of methods during a roughly six- to twelve-month period between 2021 and 2023, including interviews with paid and lay leaders; participant observation activities; surveys with congregants (though sample sizes were regrettably poor so little of this data will appear in this book); an Appreciative Inquiry event with leaders and congregants; community demographics analysis; and content analysis of various sources, such as archival records, web and social media sources, and bulletins.

As data collection occurred, the research team met several times to discuss and compare research findings, questions, analysis, and musings

---

15. Watts, *Spiritual Turn*, 153 (emphasis original).
16. Boje, "Stories," 1030.

that fed back into data analysis at the individual case study as well as larger project levels. This book is the first of what we hope will be a few collaborative monographs to arise from this research.

A common experience across our case study congregations was transition and change. We became interested in the narratives that congregations told themselves relative to these transitions, including how they interpreted, framed, approached, and ultimately flourished in ministry in the process. We heard and observed varied storylines in our research activities; however, we were struck by how deeply ingrained and consistent several of the central storylines were among those we spoke to and in the activities, observations, and documents we analyzed.

As we demonstrate in chapters 2 through 8, where we present our seven case studies, we think storyline consistency is evidence of a congregational culture and identity that has deep roots within a religious community. Storyline consistency alone does not mean a congregation will flourish; indeed, congregations can embrace a shared refrain to their peril. Still, one of our principal arguments is that storyline consistency is an important hinge to help explain congregational flourishing in the face of transition and change. From the stories that these seven congregations tell of themselves, several themes repeatedly rise to the surface to help explain congregational flourishing in the face of transition and change: visionary leadership, innovative and entrepreneurial initiatives, clear congregational identity rooted in spiritual formation, intentional systems and structures oriented toward a congregation's mission and vision, hospitable community among members, and engaged laity who collectively own and participate in the congregation's mission. Together, these factors interact with each other and help to draw members of a congregation into "our" shared story, while simultaneously and collectively cocreating a congregation's emerging story. An important outcome is collective ownership of a congregation's culture and identity—everyone singing from the same song sheet if you will—that can play a powerful role in the face of congregational transition and change. Again, these storylines reflect the complex networks, structures, relationships, and interactions across several subcultures that congregations are part of (e.g., between a congregation, denomination, and changing social context). In other words, congregations are not islands unto themselves with complete agency or autonomy to determine their fate.

Alongside the social scientific analysis that grounds this project, we also weave theological reflection and practical application throughout each chapter. Then, in chapter 9 we hear from three practitioners from across theological traditions—Archbishop Linda Nicholls, Fr. James Mallon, and Dr. Sarah Han—who provide broad theological, ecclesiological, and practical connections between the preceding chapters and diverse ministry environments. In chapter 10 we tie together common themes from the entire project, with an eye toward the theological and practical implications from this research for congregations and denominations moving forward.

The stories we tell in this volume are not representative of flourishing congregations. However, they illustrate the role of story in congregational flourishing in a way that is compatible with what we have learned about what contributes to congressional flourishing in previous research.[17] We caution against using this book in a formulaic way where you do *a*, *b*, or *c* expecting *x*, *y*, or *z* to occur. Yet, there are heuristics and tools to glean from this research that any church could contextualize to their local setting. We hope you use this book in this way.

Our deep desire is that you, the reader, will encounter a good mix of social scientific data and analysis, theological reflection, and practical application that is realistic, thought provoking, useful, and hopeful for your local ministry context.

BIBLIOGRAPHY

Ammerman, Nancy T. "Culture and Identity in the Congregation." In *Studying Congregations: A New Handbook*, edited by Nancy T. Ammerman et al., 78–104. Nashville: Abingdon, 1998.

Berger, Peter L. *Invitation to Sociology: A Humanistic Perspective*. Garden City, NY: Anchor, 1963.

Boje, David M. "Stories of the Storytelling Organization: A Postmodern Analysis of Disney as 'Tamara-Land.'" *Academy of Management Journal* 38 (1995) 997–1035. doi:10.2307/256618

———. "The Storytelling Organization: A Study of Storytelling Performance in an Office Supply Firm." *Administrative Science Quarterly* 36 (1991) 106–26.

Eliasoph, Nina, and Paul Lichterman. "Culture in Interaction." *American Journal of Sociology* 108 (2003) 735–94.

Goffman, Erving. *The Presentation of Self in Everyday Life*. Norwell, MA: Anchor, 1959.

Hopewell, James. *Congregations: Stories and Structures*. Philadelphia: Fortress, 1984.

McAlpine, Bill, et al. *Signs of Life: Catholic, Mainline, and Conservative Protestant Congregations in Canada*. Toronto, ON: Tyndale Academic, 2021.

---

17. Thiessen et al., "What Is a Flourishing Congregation"; McAlpine et al., *Signs of Life*.

Mulder, Mark T., and Gerardo Marti. *The Glass Church: Robert H. Schuller, the Crystal Cathedral, and the Strain of Megachurch Ministry*. Chicago: Rutgers University Press, 2020.

Osmer, Richard Robert. *Practical Theology: An Introduction*. Grand Rapids: Eerdmans, 2008.

Reimer, Sam, and Michael Wilkinson. *A Culture of Faith: Evangelical Congregations in Canada*. Montreal: McGill-Queen's University Press, 2015.

Schuurman, Peter J. *The Subversive Evangelical: The Ironic Charisma of an Irreligious Megachurch*. Advancing Studies in Religion 6. Montreal: McGill-Queen's University Press, 2019.

Thiessen, Joel, et al. "What Is a Flourishing Congregation? Leader Perceptions, Definitions, and Experiences." *Review of Religious Research* 61 (2018) 13–37.

Watts, Galen. *The Spiritual Turn: The Religion of the Heart and the Making of Romantic Liberal Modernity*. New York: Oxford University Press, 2022.

2

Explosively Alive
Stories of Catholic Renewal

Cathy Holtmann and Sam Reimer

WE ARRIVED EARLY TO St. Jerome's parish for the Appreciative Inquiry event, held on a rainy Tuesday evening in October 2022.[1] The goal of our Appreciative Inquiry event was to listen to the lay members describe significant events in the church's history and their memorable experiences at the parish. We wondered if many would show up. We set up tables hoping for twenty to thirty people. Soon all the tables were full, and we were scrambling to set up more. More than fifty church volunteers gave up their evening just because Father Mike had asked them to. We passed around the microphone, allowing each person to give their name and their involvement in the church. Nearly all were involved in significant and multiple ways, including leading life groups, serving the community in acts of mercy, serving as greeters or in prayer ministry, and in many other ways. We did not expect to find such high levels of lay involvement. Father Mike estimated that 50 percent of the 1,500 people who attend mass weekly were involved in ministry in the church, "which is incredible," he said. We agreed and wondered how a large Catholic parish managed to mobilize their laity to such a degree.

---

1. All names—including the names of the priest, parishioners, and parish—are pseudonyms to maintain confidentiality.

In this chapter we tell two stories that are central to the flourishing of a Catholic church in the Atlantic region. The first story is one of renewal and describes how a set of challenging circumstances at St. Jerome's Church were transformed into opportunities for re-evangelization. The second is a story of dynamic leadership in which the so-called "Game Plan" served as the template for keeping members of St. Jerome's focused on the mission of discovering Jesus, nurturing discipleship, and transforming the world. These stories emerged as deeply meaningful to the collective identity of the parish and were told to us through the case study we conducted at the parish during the summer and fall months of 2022 with the help of Misha Maitreyi, a graduate research assistant from the University of New Brunswick. During that time, we met with the parish leadership team and attended one of their monthly staff gatherings. We interviewed several staff members, current and past priests, members of the congregation, and a diocesan leader. We attended all four weekend masses, a weekday funeral, a leadership summit, and dropped in on an online life group session. We reviewed the parish website and social media channels, watched YouTube videos of homilies, and read several issues of the newsletter as well as some books published by priests associated with the parish. As noted above, we hosted a two-hour Appreciative Inquiry event to identify key periods and experiences in the parish's history, along with areas of strength and opportunities for growth. We are grateful to everyone at St. Jerome's who generously shared their experiences and knowledge of the parish with us. While the phrase "explosively alive" comes from a quote by Fr. Bob Bedard, the founder of the Companions of the Cross, the Catholic order to which the current parish priests belong, it aptly conveys the enthusiasm, hospitality, and energy that we felt during our time spent participating in liturgies and interacting with members of this congregation.[2]

STORY 1: RENEWAL

Historical Context

The context for the story of St. Jerome's renewal begins with a challenging set of circumstances. Like many Catholic dioceses across North America in the last fifty years, the one in which St. Jerome's is located was experiencing decline in the number of Catholics engaged in local churches. According

---

2. Bedard, quoted on "About Us."

to data from the Canadian census, the proportion of Canadians identifying as Catholic fell from 46 percent to 30 percent between 1971 and 2021.[3] In Atlantic Canada, that proportion is currently about 32 percent.[4] Atlantic Canadians are more likely to identify as religious than people in other regions of the country. However, we know that religious affiliation is not the same as religious participation, and that too has declined over the years. In the Atlantic region, there are substantial variations in regular religious participation between generations, with younger people less likely to attend mass regularly than older generations of Catholics.[5] Declining numbers of engaged Catholics means less money in parish collection plates. In 2004, the diocese launched an initiative for amalgamations because the number of churches was unsustainable.

Around the same time that the amalgamation process was announced, allegations of clergy sexual abuse of children in the diocese surfaced. In the following years, several priests were criminally convicted of sexually abusing children as far back as the 1960s. A class action suit against the diocese was launched in 2018, based on claims that the diocese had a decades-long policy of secrecy concerning allegations of sexual abuse against a priest. The claim for $10 million was settled in November 2022.[6] While the extensive media coverage of clergy sexual abuse locally and around the globe was presumably one of multiple factors that contributed to the decline in engagement among Catholics in the diocese,[7] more significantly, clergy sexual abuse crimes contributed to a fundamental "violation of meaning" for many.[8] The Catholic sacramental worldview asserts that sacraments effect what they signify—"ordinary things and people manifest the presence and saving activity of God."[9] Sacraments are central to the religious identity of most Catholics. The crimes of sexual abuse committed by priests and their cover-up by bishops call the Catholic sacramental worldview into question. Catholics questioning the meaning of their faith and their trust in leadership in the light of crimes of clergy sexual abuse may also have stopped coming to church.

3 Statistics Canada, "Canadian Census."
4. Statistics Canada, "Canadian Census."
5. Cornelissen, *Religiosity*, 12.
6. Supreme Court of Nova Scotia, *Gallant v. Roman Catholic*, para. 1.
7. Ballano, "Catholic Laity," 4.
8. Guido, "Unique Betrayal," 255.
9. Guido, "Unique Betrayal," 260.

The final element that set the stage for renewal at St. Jerome's was the rise in the number of immigrants choosing to settle in the Atlantic region. This was the result of provincial government efforts to stimulate population growth in the region. They partnered with Immigration, Refugee, and Citizenship Canada (IRCC) to create provincial nominee programs to attract immigrants to meet labor market demands. The Atlantic Immigration Pilot Program and the Atlantic Immigration Program have coordinated provincial efforts to increase immigration of skilled workers and international students to the region.[10] The share of immigrants settling in Atlantic Canada has almost tripled, rising from 1.2 percent in 2006 to 3.5 percent in 2021.[11] Compared to the rest of the country, this probably seems quite low, but this change in population demographics has been noticeable in the region's cities, including the city of our case study. In fact, the neighborhood in which St. Jerome's is located is attractive to large numbers of immigrants. That is why at the time of the amalgamation of the three Catholic churches in the area into St. Jerome's, the diocese agreed to build a new building for St. Jerome's, anticipating growth.

These three elements of the local context, declining numbers of engaged Catholics, the devastating impacts of clergy sexual abuse, and the rising numbers of immigrants, are certainly disruptive and potentially problematic. These elements converged and resulted in the birth of a new Catholic parish in a new $9.5-million building. The priest who led the congregation through this period of change framed this challenging set of circumstances as an opportunity for a new beginning and renewal. According to one of the early pastors at St. Jerome's, the process was "guided by prayers and consultation." The amalgamation wasn't just about pooling resources from three separate churches but involved a willingness to try new things, a "new way of being new." This is reflective of "innovation" in the Flourishing Congregations Construct introduced in the last chapter (fig. 1.1). St. Jerome's is referred to by diocesan staff as a pastoral laboratory. For many parishioners this was an exciting "grace-filled" time of change. Of course, not everyone was happy; some felt forced into this merger with another parish. Nevertheless, the story of renewal propelled the new parish forward.

---

10. "Atlantic Immigration Program," para. 1.
11. Statistics Canada, "Immigrants," para. 33.

The New Evangelization

The process of renewal at St. Jerome's was centered on the mission of the global Catholic Church to evangelize disciples for Christ. This mission is not new, but the discourse of the "New Evangelization" is and was made popular by Pope John Paul II in the early 1990s.[12] By virtue of their baptism in Christ, all Catholics are invited to witness to their faith in whatever circumstances or vocations they find themselves. The New Evangelization is focused both externally on people who have not yet encountered Christ and internally on "re-proposing" the gospel to Catholics who have experienced a crisis of faith. Typically, Catholic parishes have a small core of people who are highly engaged and a large proportion of people at the periphery.[13] The latter include Catholics who only attend mass on holidays and to celebrate rites of passage like baptisms, weddings, and funerals. The New Evangelization movement resulted in the emergence of new Catholic men's and women's groups throughout North America, as well as a broad network of "conferences, and television, radio and internet-based media venues."[14] The New Evangelization movement draws from evangelical Protestant sensibilities and language, elements of the Catholic charismatic movement, and an emphasis on a personal relationship with Jesus.[15] In promoting the New Evangelization, the Canadian Conference of Catholic Bishops (CCCB) emphasized a "new enthusiasm, new methods and new expression" capable of involving all people, "no matter the color of skin, language, or ethnic origin."[16] The Canadian bishops highlighted the necessity of collaboration between Catholic clergy and laity in this process of renewal.

St. Jerome's is an example of the New Evangelization in action. An early pastor at St. Jerome's has written critically of the "maintenance" mode of many Catholic churches. He describes this as a culture of unhealthy attitudes and behaviors such as traditionally minded Catholics who believe if they fulfil their obligation to go to mass, be nice and say their prayers, God will let them into heaven; postmodern Catholics who pursue a self-centered spirituality of autonomy and niceness; neo-pelagians who seek to recover a lost past through moral and disciplinary rigorism; and clericalism, which

---

12. McCallion et al., "Individualism and Community," 292.
13. Adler et al., *American Parishes*, 238–39.
14. McCallion et al., "Individualism and Community," 292.
15. "Evangelization, Catechesis, Catholic Education."
16. Gervais, "New Evangelization," 12.

disempowers the laity from experiencing their baptismal identity in Jesus and serving the body of Christ. He argues that churches need to refocus on revitalizing the mature engagement of Catholics at the parish level through responding to the signs of the times, changing their pastoral methods, and focusing on the church as an institutional force for social good. In this model of renewal, lay ministry involves "serving the poor, feeding the hungry, evangelizing and forming small Christian communities."[17] In our study of St. Jerome's, we observed two main drivers for this mission of re-engagement: Alpha and Sunday mass.

Alpha

Everyone at St. Jerome's is invited to enroll in an Alpha course, regardless of how long they have identified as Catholic. According to the Alpha Canada—Catholic Context website, Alpha is a tool for parish evangelization based on hospitality, sharing, and open conversation. It consists of eleven weekly meetings, which include a meal, a talk, and time for small group reflection. The program also includes a retreat and a celebration dinner.[18] Alpha is part of a strategy for changing Catholic culture, shifting the focus toward adult evangelization. Two staff members at St. Jerome's coordinate Alpha, training lay leaders who run multiple programs throughout the year. The parish leadership aim for a 50 percent turnover in Alpha group leaders from year to year, so that laity who identify as disciples can take on leadership roles in other parish ministries.

One recent graduate of St. Jerome's Alpha program said, "Alpha was life-changing for me," because she grew a lot in her faith. She emphasized, "The [Alpha] retreat was very like filling for me. . . . That emptiness in your heart and everything. . . . Oh, the Holy Spirit was there for me answering the questions I had." Alpha is not only intended to renew cradle Catholics' relationship with God but deepen their relationships with other members of the parish who have had similar experiences of a rekindled faith. Alpha at St. Jerome's also fosters a culture of hospitality for those who come to explore the Catholic faith. It invites Catholics to expand the circle of people they care about.[19] People can experience a sense of belonging to the church community, ask some of the big questions about life, and listen to

---

17. Mallon, *Divine Renovation*, 70–83.
18. "Equipping Your Parish," paras. 1, 5.
19. Huntley and Mallon, *Unlocking Your Parish*, 40.

the experiences of Catholics before they are asked to believe the teachings of the church and participate in its sacraments.[20] "Over time, people learn how to pray for one another, which then becomes an integral part of life in the parish."[21]

Post-Alpha, the relationships and prayer practices nurtured in individuals are further supported through regular participation in life groups. The pastor at St. Jerome's described the format for life group meetings:

> The essence of [life groups include] three qualities—where people can connect, grow, and pray. So, some elements of human connection—fellowship or whatever—it could involve a meal or an ice breaker or something to that effect to connect, to grow. Then there's a growth component. So whether they're following a video series or doing a book study or somebody within the group is giving a talk but there's a sense of "I wanna grow deeper in prayer and my relationship with God," maybe understanding Scripture or church teaching, [or] what have you, and then to pray in some form of communal prayer.

He estimates that, of the 1,500 people that attend mass weekly or watch online, about 500 parishioners meet regularly in life groups. We met the members of an online life group that people from St. Jerome's and Catholics in South Asia formed during the COVID-19 pandemic. They described their experiences as life-changing and, according to one member, St. Jerome's church is "a light on a hill." Life group members have access to online resources through the parish's subscription to Formed.[22] The pastor refers to this as "the Netflix of Catholic content." It features thousands of videos, books, programs, and audio related to Catholicism. Life group members' access to online tools for independent learning increases their understanding and engagement with their faith and the wider church. The small group model of Alpha and life groups helps individual Catholics at St. Jerome's to develop a deeper level of engagement with their faith and with other parishioners. In effect, they are becoming disciples. As a result of regular, intentional, and intimate faith-sharing experiences, people come to expect the same quality of engagement in other areas of parish life.

---

20. Ireland, "Effectiveness of Process Evangelism," 2.
21. Alpha Canada, "Catholic Context," 6.
22. Formed, "Welcome to Formed."

Sunday Mass

The experience of Sunday mass—with a focus on hospitality, high quality music, and effective preaching—is another key piece of the renewal process at St. Jerome's. The parish leadership team prioritizes "preparing for and celebrating the Sunday Eucharist to make it the best possible experience for the maximum number of people."[23] Parish leaders make it clear that Catholics should not just show up to mass expecting to be served but to serve; they are not guests but hosts. According to the current priest, "dozens and dozens of people" are involved in preparing for and celebrating each liturgy, one of which is live streamed on Facebook. The parish started live streaming mass in 2014 and was the first Catholic church in the diocese to do so, harnessing technology and social media as tools for evangelization. One lay leader emphasized that the quality of the live stream mass on Facebook is important because it may be a viewer's first impression of St. Jerome's. Sunday mass is *the* most important opportunity for the leadership at St. Jerome's to convey the vision of the church and its story of individual and collective renewal so that the language of evangelization is shared and the congregational culture is changed.

The four weekend masses feature different liturgical styles. Everyone who comes through the church doors is greeted with a warm welcome by ministers of hospitality wearing name tags. The foyer is large, bright, and conducive to socializing. The two Sunday morning masses are the most popular with high quality, live, contemporary Christian music accompanied by combinations of acoustic guitars, electric guitars, keyboard, and drums. On the morning we visited two of the songs were in the top ten of SongSelect by Christian Copyright Licensing International (CCLI).[24] People sway to the music, singing with their hands in the air, and children dance in the aisles—this is not a typical experience of a Catholic mass. The Saturday evening liturgy features more traditional Catholic songs and hymns. The Sunday evening mass is contemplative with Latin chants, dimmed lighting, and more candles. The sanctuary's two large screens, one on either side of the altar, are highly visible. The screens draw everyone's attention forward with a few appropriate and strategically placed images along with text for prayers and song lyrics.

---

23. Mallon, *Divine Renovation*, 96.
24. CCLI, SongSelect.

Effective preaching is a priority for priests at St. Jerome's. One priest commented, "The need for strategic preaching that pierces hearts, inspires personal conversion to Jesus, unleashes missionary disciples, and helps the parish to break out of maintenance has never been greater."[25] Priests work with the parish leadership team to brainstorm topics for preaching series throughout the liturgical year. Each weekend mass features one priest preaching the same homily, which is well-crafted with an easy-to-understand theme rooted in the lectionary Scriptures, along with personal examples and memorable messages such as "the parish is a people praying with a purpose." Thematic preaching gives parishioners an idea of what to expect from week-to-week and retain what they have learned.[26]

Our experience of weekend liturgies at St. Jerome's were feelings of high welcome and shared community rather than an exclusive celebration of the sacrament of communion. The message of welcome was expressed in a variety of ways beyond the ministry of hospitality, including the accessibility of the congregation's responses to the liturgical prayers and song lyrics on the big screens, the high-quality sound system, the priest's genuine engagement with in-person and online participants, and the large number of people singing tuneful songs. Folks were not rushing out the doors after communion but lingering over coffee and conversation in the foyer long after the last note of the closing song. Liturgical renewal at St. Jerome's, while thoroughly compliant with Catholic sacrament practice, is spiritually and emotionally engaging members of the parish as Catholic disciples in the body of Christ.

STORY 2: LEADERSHIP

The second storyline focuses on leadership. As we will see in the case studies to follow, visionary leadership is necessary for congregational flourishing.[27] Leaders articulate a shared vision, which shapes the direction of the parish. They are relational, energizing lay involvement. They are innovative, helping their congregation adapt to changing realities. Previous congregational research in Canada asked denominational leaders and church planters what distinguishes flourishing congregations from those that are not flourishing, and the most common response was courageous, visionary

---

25. Colautti et al. *Preaching on Purpose*, loc. 183.
26. Lobo, *Divine Renovation Apprentice*, 35–37.
27. McAlpine et al., *Signs of Life*.

leadership.²⁸ Research confirms that nearly all indicators of congregational flourishing are related to a leadership style that is collaborative and which inspires the laity to make decisions.²⁹ St. Jerome's is no exception. Their pastors are *religious institutional entrepreneurs*. Gerardo Marti defines religious institutional entrepreneurs as "actors who seek to change institutional arrangements by mobilizing people and other resources to transform existing institutions and create new ones."³⁰ In the words of an early pastor, their task was to move congregants from "maintenance to mission"—which is no small task. Below we present three qualities of entrepreneurial religious leadership that we witnessed at St. Jerome's. While this is not an exhaustive list, we are suggesting that these leader qualities are important, possibly necessary, to move any congregation from maintaining the status quo to being "explosively alive." These qualities are the ability to train and mobilize lay leaders, to provide innovative leadership through change, and to create structures and processes to support ministry.

Mobilizing Lay Leadership

The current priest shortage in the Catholic Church in Canada means that each priest oversees a greater number of laity and sometimes has multiple parishes under their leadership.³¹ They cannot do all the needed ministry alone, so they must mobilize the laity. St. Jerome's first pastor was described by his successor as "a visionary leader," who had a "great ability to see the giftedness in other people, mobilize them, and give real responsibility and authority to people." Parishioners evinced a deep bond with their priests, describing these relationships as displaying a "special connection." This was not a case of a charismatic leader having power over a passive laity. Rather, it was about leaders communicating a new vision that the lay members internalized, and it was about trust in the priest's leadership. They wanted to get involved. Laity were moved from spectators to co-owners of St. Jerome's mission, reflecting the "engaged laity" dimension of the Flourishing Congregations Construct.

Of course, lay leaders must be trained for ministry. St. Jerome's hosts three leadership summits per year with an average of seventy to one

28. Reimer and Wilkinson, *Culture of Faith*, 135.
29. Carroll, *God's Potters*.
30. Marti, "New Concepts," 8.
31. Bibby and Reid, *Canada's Catholics*, 147.

hundred lay persons attending each time. The summit we observed was well structured, including prayer, music, visuals, a vision talk, and a time for participants to learn about and practice a leadership skill. The priest emphasized that God leads the work and lay leaders make possible all ministries at St. Jerome's. A three-step process for leadership development was explained: (1) pray daily, (2) look for opportunities to develop leadership in others, and (3) ask someone to become a leader. In describing the process of inviting new people into leadership, reference was made to the theme of a recent preaching series: leaders had asked others to "pick up an oar" (see Luke 5:10).

Some who were formerly lay volunteers are now paid staff. They are empowered to make important decisions on their own, and they are commissioned to recruit volunteers for their area of ministry. They recruit laity as greeters, musicians, lectors, Eucharistic ministers, children and youth ministers, small group leaders, video and sound technicians, and much more. Over half of the parish staff team are women, and some current paid lay ministers were attracted to the parish from Protestant churches. All are encouraged to serve.

Innovation

Second, innovation—another characteristic within the Flourishing Congregations Construct—is an important dimension of good leadership. In a rapidly changing society, churches must adapt, and leaders must lead through change. When we began gathering data on St. Jerome's, it was still recovering from the COVID-19 lockdowns. During COVID, churches were not able to meet in person, and as a result, attendance plummeted and volunteers stopped serving. When we arrived in 2022, attendance was increasing and new people were joining, even though attendance was still below pre-COVID levels. What helped St. Jerome's recovery was initiatives that started prior to the pandemic. As noted above, the parish started live streaming the 9:00 a.m. Sunday service in 2014. Their online presentation improved during COVID lockdowns, as leaders learned new skills for engaging a virtual audience. During our observation of the live stream mass in 2022, the celebrant addressed both in-person and online attendees throughout. For example, he invited online viewers to type their prayer intentions into the comments on Facebook. St. Jerome's staff were also instrumental in helping other parishes develop an online presence during the lockdowns. The point is that St. Jerome's was well positioned for the changes brought on by the pandemic because of innovative initiatives prior to the pandemic.

St. Jerome's harnesses a variety of digital and conventional platforms to communicate with parishioners and people beyond the parish boundaries, including its website, email, social media—including Facebook, X (formerly Twitter) and Instagram—YouTube videos, as well as printed magazines, posters, and books. During the pandemic, small groups, like Alpha and life groups, continued to meet via Zoom. Children's ministries moved online with video-recorded Sunday school classes. Overall, the quality of its communications is high. As mentioned above, the four weekend masses are diverse and innovative in presentation, while maintaining the structure of the Catholic liturgy. The diverse styles attract a diverse crowd, including many recent immigrants and young families.

Structures and Processes

Innovation does not stop with newer technology or engaging Sunday services. Innovative structures and processes are needed as well, spearheaded by visionary leaders. The third important component of visionary leadership is the ability to develop structures that maintain and support the mission of the parish, which, in turn, support a positive "organizational ethos," another quality from the Flourishing Congregations Construct.

During the early years of St. Jerome's, the parish was growing quickly, the priest was away traveling often, and the limited staff were overwhelmed and near burnout. The priest realized the parish needed to restructure, and he called in an external consultant to examine their current practices and help them make the necessary changes. The result involved hiring staff to support the volunteers so they could thrive. Flourishing parishes are not those where the staff do all the work but where the paid staff complete the background tasks (e.g., accounting, scheduling, arranging songs, planning children's curricula, training laity) that allow volunteers to be empowered to work well. The St. Jerome's leadership is not afraid to draw on expertise from outside the Catholic tradition, particularly in areas where Catholics have been historically less active, like in children's ministry or Alpha courses.

Good structures and processes are needed to assure that all activities within the parish are directed to further the vision of the parish. If programs or systems no longer contribute to the mission of making disciples, then they are using up valuable time and money and should end. For example, one staff member noted that they decided not to provide the lay-requested live streams of funerals, weddings, and so forth, because these live streams do not fulfill the mission of making disciples but only serve the people who are already involved. Removing old structures and refusing lay requests, however, are often costly. Those parishioners who want to keep the traditions of their parish may become unhappy, stop giving and volunteering, or even leave. Yet, trust in leadership is also built when laity know that the time and money they invest in the parish is used strategically to fulfill the mission they embrace.

Lastly, good structures mean that there are plenty of "on-ramps" toward involvement and spiritual growth. New attenders receive an enthusiastic and warm welcome, drawing them into relationships and parish life. As noted above, adult congregants are expected to actively pursue opportunities for spiritual growth and service, like attending Alpha and joining a life group. Those parents who seek sacraments like baptism, first communion, or catechism classes for their children are expected to stay and fully participate as a family in preparatory classes—they cannot drop the kids off and leave. Finally, children and youth ministries provide the processes that allow the next generation to stay involved in the parish during young adulthood. For example, the children's minister told us that her former Sunday school children were helping run the daily Vacation Bible School that summer.

In sum, leadership changed the culture in the parish. The process was not easy. Some Catholics left who preferred the old ways of doing church. But as the former pastor said of those who left, "We never really had them anyway." Iannaccone and others have suggested that demanding churches rule out "free riders"—those pew-warmers who contribute little to the congregation—often because it promotes a "costly" faith that is in tension with the society.[32] Yet St. Jerome's leadership has managed to create a culture of high involvement even while remaining welcoming to all. Two aspects of the changed congregational culture stood out to us as external observers: the level of lay engagement and the commitment to the Game Plan, which laid out the means to reaching their vision.

One priest told us that the priests "set the culture" by communicating "high expectation" that all laity should attend, give, and serve. The parish—he teaches from the pulpit—is like a "family business so we're all co-owners." The leaders worked hard to change the idea that "you are doing us a favor" when you attend; instead, the expectation is that you both attend

---

32. Iannaccone, "Strict Churches," 1181.

weekly and contribute to the corporate work of the parish. He shared that, prior to COVID, "There would have been a point where I would say well over 50 percent of people—like every other person [who] would come to a mass on a Sunday was involved in ministry, which is incredible." It was clear from our interviews and the Appreciative Inquiry event (recounted above) that laity were buying into the vision and were actively volunteering and giving. The interviewees would often quote what they had heard from the clergy. The message was getting through to the people in the pews. One staff member noted that the previous priest would "call people out" (not individuals, but "the type" of attendee) who would leave right after communion and not serve in the parish. No one was to be an observer; everyone was called to be part of the mission.

The resulting strength of the culture of lay engagement is hard to overstate. One staff member said that he was "pulled in" to volunteer service because "everyone was doing it." A volunteer said that there were people in the church volunteering full time in unpaid positions. St. Jerome's, she stated, would post an unpaid job and they would be "bombarded with applications." She went on to say: "When I'm at the end of my career, I hope that I can go and give back that way, because, you know, they're just wonderful, warm, giving, faithful people. You know, I would love to be like them."

Yet, despite the relatively high level of lay engagement, the parish leadership wanted to do better. A priest shared,

> I think one of the internal questions we're wrestling with . . . [is] are we actually making disciples? . . . [There is] the sacramental understanding of being saved at baptism but then oftentimes that's in infancy and so there's an unpacking of those graces in time and very often somebody needs to ratify the decision of their parents later in life, and whether it's a teenager, young adult or later still, where they take ownership for that and say yes to Jesus. . . . We're doing pretty good, but I would say for a church of our size with the resources that we have, I would love to see us like seeing hundreds and hundreds of people coming to relationship with Jesus in a much more significant way.

At St. Jerome's the measure of lay engagement was more than just tracking the number of people involved in ministry, it also encompassed the depth of their discipleship.

One of the traits of flourishing congregations is that the leaders and people in the pews know who they are and what the parish is about.[33] They are committed to working together to fulfill the shared mission. At St. Jerome's, how the vision is realized is captured in the Game Plan. The Game Plan is visible throughout St. Jerome's building on large posters and in the literature on display. It invites people to participate in a process—"discover Jesus, grow together, worship God, serve others, and go out." This clear, simple plan guides attendees through steps toward greater discipleship: discovering Jesus through Alpha, growing together through life groups, worshipping God through regularly attending and giving financially at Sunday mass, serving others in the church community, and going out to evangelize and perform acts of mercy. More importantly, the Game Plan is not just a plaque on the wall that was created sometime in the past and is now largely ignored. Staff and laity we talked to were able to articulate the Game Plan. In fact, our interviewees were able to articulate the mission of the parish using similar language—the language they had heard from the priests. Shared language is one of the best indicators of a strong congregational culture.[34]

The story of St. Jerome's is one of transformation. It is a story of a process of Catholic renewal that resulted in a church that is explosively alive. It is a story of a small group of leaders who saw barriers to flourishing—declining attendance, a sexual abuse scandal, expensive buildings in need of upkeep—as opportunities to start something new. We have argued that the central catalyst behind this transformation is visionary leadership. Leaders envisioned the amalgamation of three parishes into one, but the new parish was more than the sum of the three parts. It was more than just a new, attractive building. It was a new building with a new vision. Many Catholic dioceses are amalgamating parishes, but many of these newly amalgamated churches decline because the laity are not energized by a compelling vision. Leaders must promote a clear vision, and if successful, the laity internalize that vision, claiming it as their own.

When churches flourish, they can grow quickly. If leadership do not adapt (even transform) the organizational structure and processes to keep up with the growth, the church will flounder as people burn out and tasks are left undone. Visionary leaders are innovative, adjusting to growth and the changing environment. When the leaders at St. Jerome's were in over their heads, they reached out for external help. They made changes to

---

33. McAlpine et al., *Signs of Life*.
34. Ammerman et al., *Studying Congregations*, 168–69.

properly support the ministry, funneling resources to new areas as needed. One priest told us that no church is healthy enough to withstand bad leadership. Yes, strong leadership is central to the St. Jerome's story.

So how does the story of St. Jerome's help your church move from maintaining the status quo to becoming explosively alive? One key for St. Jerome's was the ability of leaders to see an opportunity for a fresh start in the midst of difficult circumstances. Declining attendance, old buildings that are costly to maintain, a sexual abuse scandal, and changing demographics could easily have been seen as insurmountable barriers to flourishing. Yet, the visionary leaders saw it as an opportunity to make a clean break from the past and start a new work with renewed energy and a new vision. How would your congregation respond to difficult circumstances like these?

Fresh starts require leaving the old behind, and the leaders avoided some pitfalls that could have led to failure. With the support of the diocese, they wisely chose to build a new facility, even at considerable expense. If they had decided to close two of the three amalgamating parishes and renovate the third, the likely result would have been a continuation of the ethos of that (declining) parish. In this scenario, the new vision could be undermined by parishioners who would be disgruntled because their building was not selected to be preserved. The new building in a new location not only facilitated a new start, but the structure was built for a new approach to ministry: the large vestibule or foyer is ideal as a welcoming and community-building space, the nave features amphitheater-style seating for seven hundred people and good lighting, and the audio-visual technology and team are coordinated from a balcony overlooking the nave and sanctuary. In addition, a new pastor was brought in by the bishop. The new priest wanted to try something new. He had a new plan and the new parish became an experimental laboratory for a new vision. Sometimes a clean break from the past—which may include new leadership and even a new space—is required to move from decline to flourishing.

The hard part is getting the laity from the declining parishes on board so they commit to the new vision. How can leaders lead laity to commit to something new? For a successful transition, it was important that parishioners at St. Jerome's were involved in the discernment process; they worked with clergy to set a new course. Their input in the process allowed them to "own" the new vision and get on board. Of course, not everyone got on board. Some left because they preferred the old way, which was comfortable and made minimal demands.

A major transition like that of St. Jerome's requires more than mobilizing laity. Since trying something new is a risk, with considerable costs, denominational or diocesan leaders must support the new pastor during what will inevitably be a rocky start. It also requires new systems and structures that allow congregational goals to be reached. As noted above, "on-ramps" were created to draw people into greater involvement and discipleship. The parish's Game Plan clearly communicates the prescribed means to the desired goals. Necessary resources—money and staff—were put in place to properly support the Game Plan, while those tasks peripheral to the parish's goals were ended.

Does your church have a game plan that is streamlined to lead newcomers toward greater involvement and discipleship? Is it simple for congregants to understand? Is it compelling? Is it promoted enough for the laity to commit to it? Do peripheral programs or processes need to be removed? Asking such questions can help your church become "explosively alive."

QUESTIONS FOR REFLECTION

1. How might your church create "on-ramps" to draw people into greater commitment? Would Alpha or life groups work in your setting?
2. St. Jerome's parish attempts to measure growth in discipleship by tracking measures of religiosity among lay attendees, including involvement in the parish, private devotionalism, evangelization, etc. Do you think it is possible to measure discipleship growth in this way? Would it work in your setting to collect such data?
3. Does your congregation have adequate staff in place to flourish? How would you be able to tell?
4. Does your church need a change in culture? What would it take for such a change to occur?

BIBLIOGRAPHY

Adler, Gary J., et al., eds. *American Parishes: Remaking Local Catholicism.* New York: Fordham University Press, 2019.

Alpha Canada. "Equipping Your Parish in Its Mission to Help People Discover Jesus." https://alphacanada.org/catholic-context/.

———. "An Introduction to Alpha, Catholic Context: Equipping Parishes in Their Mission to Help People Encounter Jesus." https://alphacanada.org/wp-content/uploads/2023/06/Alpha-Canada-Catholics-Intro-Guide-Soplit-Page-2023.pdf.

Ammerman, Nancy T., et al. *Studying Congregations: A New Handbook*. Nashville: Abingdon, 1998.

Ballano, Vivencio O. "The Catholic Laity, Clerical Sexual Abuse, and Married Priesthood: A Sociological Analysis of Vatican II's Lay Empowerment." *Cogent Social Sciences* 6 (2020). https://doi.org/10.1080/23311886.2020.1813438.

Bibby, Reginald W., and Angus Reid. *Canada's Catholics: Vitality and Hope in a New Era*. Ottawa, ON: Novalis, 2016.

Canadian Conference of Catholic Bishops. "Evangelization, Catechesis, Catholic Education." https://www.cccb.ca/evangelization-catechesis-catholic-education/.

Carroll, Jackson W. *God's Potters: Pastoral Leadership and the Shaping of Congregations*. Grand Rapids: Eerdmans, 2006.

Christian Copyright Licensing International (CCLI). SongSelect. https://songselect.ccli.com/.

Colautti, Alex, et al. *Preaching on Purpose: A Divine Renovation Handbook for Communicating the Gospel Today*. Halifax, NS: Divine Renovation Ministry, 2022. Kindle.

Companions of the Cross. "About Us: Unite." https://companionscross.org/about-us/.

Cornelissen, Louis. *Religiosity in Canada and Its Evolution from 1985 to 2019*. Statistics Canada, Insights on Canadian Society, Oct. 28, 2021. https://www150.statcan.gc.ca/n1/pub/75-006-x/2021001/article/00010-eng.htm.

Formed. "Welcome to Formed: The Premier Catholic Streaming Service." Augustine Institute and Ignatius Press. www.formed.org.

Gervais, Michael A. J. "Towards a New Evangelization: Message by the Permanent Council of the Canadian Conference of Catholic Bishops on the 500th Anniversary of the Evangelization of the Americas." Canadian Conference of Catholic Bishops, Sept. 14, 1992. https://www.cccb.ca/wp-content/uploads/2020/04/42.-Toward-a-New-Evangn-500th_anniv_Christopher_Columbus.pdf.

Government of Canada. "Atlantic Immigration Program." Immigration and Citizenship, Government of Canada, last updated May 15, 2024. https://www.canada.ca/en/immigration-refugees-citizenship/services/immigrate-canada/atlantic-immigration.html.

Guido, Joseph J. "A Unique Betrayal: Clergy Sexual Abuse in the Context of the Catholic Religious Tradition." *Journal of Child Sexual Abuse*, 17.3–4 (2008) 255–69.

Huntley, Ron, and James Mallon. *Unlocking Your Parish: Making Disciples, Raising Up Leaders with Alpha*. Frederick, MD: Word Among Us, 2019.

Iannaccone, Laurence R. "Why Strict Churches Are Strong." *American Journal of Sociology*, 99 (1994) 1180–211.

Ireland, Mark. "A Study of the Effectiveness of Process Evangelism Courses in the Diocese of Lichfield, with Special Reference to *Alpha*." Master's thesis, Cliff College, 2000.

Lobo, Simon. *Divine Renovation Apprentice: Learning to Lead a Disciple-Making Parish*. Frederick, MD: Word Among Us, 2018.

Mallon, James. *Divine Renovation: Bringing Your Parish from Maintenance to Mission*. Frederick, MD: Twenty-Third, 2014.

Marti, Gerardo. "New Concepts for New Dynamics: Generating Theory for the Study of Religious Innovation and Change," *Journal for the Scientific Study of Religion* 56 (2017) 6–18.

McAlpine, Bill, et al. *Signs of Life: Catholic, Mainline, and Conservative Protestant Congregations in Canada*. Toronto: Tyndale Academic, 2021.

McCallion, Michael J., et al. "Individualism and Community as Contested Rhetorics in the Catholic New Evangelization Movement." *Review of Religious Research* 54 (2012) 291–310.

Reimer, Sam, and Michael Wilkinson. *A Culture of Faith: Evangelical Congregations in Canada*. Montreal: McGill-Queen's University Press, 2015.

Statistics Canada. "The Canadian Census: A Rich Portrait of the Country's Religious and Ethnocultural Diversity." Oct. 26, 2022. www150.statcan.gc.ca/n1/daily-quotidien/221026/dq221026b-eng.htm.

———. "Census Profile: 2021 Census of Population." Last updated Nov. 15, 2023. https://www12.statcan.gc.ca/census-recensement/2021/dp-pd/prof/index.cfm?Lang=E.

———. "Immigrants Make Up the Largest Share of the Population in Over 150 Years and Continue to Shape Who We Are as Canadians." *The Daily*, Oct. 26, 2022. https://www150.statcan.gc.ca/n1/daily-quotidien/221026/dq221026a-eng.htm.

Supreme Court of Nova Scotia. *Gallant v. The Roman Catholic Episcopal Corporation of Halifax*. 2022 NSSC 347. Dec. 5, 2022. https://kmlaw.ca/wp-content/uploads/2022/12/IA_Reasons_for_Decision_Settlement-Approval_rendered_December_5_2022.pdf.

3

Cultivating Repertoires of Resilience
Storying Challenges and Change Towards Future Flourishing

Katie Steeves, Jason John Burtt, and Michael Wilkinson

INTRODUCTION

ST. EUSTACE'S IS A medium-sized Anglican congregation in the greater Vancouver region with a strong reputation for flourishing in the areas of spiritual development and community engagement, as well as inclusivity and authenticity.[1] They meet for regular Sunday morning services and offer a wealth of programs for parishioners and the community from their church building, including the activities of their center for spiritual renewal, weekly community meals, and a kids' church program. Other community organizations also regularly use their building throughout the week, and so St. Eustace's could be aptly described as a hub of activity and resources for the parish.

Our research team, composed of the three authors of this chapter, attended services, interviewed nine member and leaders, and conducted a focus group between November of 2021 and September of 2022. Members of the team also attended church weeknight events during this time, including

---

1. Pseudonyms are used for the congregation and participants in this chapter.

the kids' church program and the weekly community meal. During our Sunday morning visits, attendance averaged around fifty to seventy-five people on a Sunday, and the services continued to be live streamed to allow others to participate online. While "re-flourishing" (as one congregation member said) in the wake of the COVID-19 pandemic was front of mind for St. Eustace's during the time frame of our case study, we quickly discovered that COVID-19 was not the first challenging circumstance they had encountered. Learning about this congregation's history led us to reflect on how flourishing might occur not just in spite of, but actually *through* experiencing difficult circumstances, changes, and transitions.

In this chapter, we use examples from the St. Eustace's case study to develop our concept of "repertoires of resilience," which we hope might be useful for other congregations. These repertoires are composed of the stories and symbols organizations use, in an aspirational way, for framing challenging moments in their history toward future possibility and flourishing. While different congregations may define flourishing in diverse ways, we draw on the Flourishing Congregations Construct outlined in chapter one. When placed within this framework, the repertoires of resilience concept may help illuminate some of the processes behind developing a healthy "organizational ethos,"[2] specifically the cultivation of church identity, strength of leadership, and willingness to innovate and change during pivotal times. Our hope is that, through learning from St. Eustace's, other congregations from a variety of denominations and contexts might consider the intentional ways they could cultivate repertoires of resilience to frame challenges in their own circumstances, histories, and contexts toward flourishing.

STORIES, CULTURE, RESILIENCE

Stories are central to framing how people come to understand and make sense of themselves and the world around them, on both an individual and organizational level.[3] Through storytelling, both the teller(s) and listener(s) work together to shape how past and present events are understood, which may open (or close) possible paths forward for the future.[4] Such stories can be communicated verbally but also through actions, the display of symbols, and histories, or through communications contained in organizational

---

2. McAlpine et al., *Signs of Life*, 19.
3. Somers, "Constitution of Identity."
4. Boje, "Stories"; Somers, "Constitution of Identity"; Swidler, "Culture in Action."

documents and websites. Cultural stories about who we are, where we have been, and what our purpose form a part of what Ann Swidler calls a cultural "tool kit" that individuals and organizations (like religious congregations) have at their disposal for a variety of purposes, such as helping to solve problems.[5] Reflecting on the power of such storytelling, Margaret Somers suggests,

> People are guided to act in certain ways, and not others, on the basis of the projections, expectations, and memories derived from a multiplicity but ultimately limited repertoire of available social, public, and cultural narratives.[6]

The stories we tell then, whether intentionally cultivated or reproduced without reflection, can have the power to guide and shape the actions of others. This makes stories an important institutional cultural tool, as storytelling can provide a resource to orient a community toward flourishing even in the midst of challenging circumstances. Among racialized communities facing oppression, for example, narratives have been shown to offer a type of "aspirational capital" they can draw from that produces community cultural wealth.[7] Aspirational capital "refers to the ability to maintain hopes and dreams for the future, even in the face of real and perceived barriers."[8] It exists when groups tell stories that "nurture a culture of possibility" even in the midst of real disadvantage.[9]

Our analysis of case study data from St. Eustace's church inspired our related concept, "repertoires of resilience," which we believe can be applied to a broader range of groups and religious congregations. We picture these repertoires as being like cultural multi-tools of aspirational stories, processes, and symbols that people can draw from to promote resilience, endurance, and flourishing when facing challenges or uncertainty. Our case study data suggests that if repertoires of resilience are cultivated collaboratively by church leadership and members, congregations can reap real benefits through communally approaching difficult circumstances from a position of possibility as opposed to embodying stories of deficit or defeat.

---

5. Swidler, "Culture in Action," 273.
6. Somers, "Constitution of Identity," 614.
7. Yosso, "Culture Has Capital," 77
8. Yosso, "Culture Has Capital," 78.
9. Yosso, "Culture Has Capital," 78.

ST. EUSTACE'S HISTORY: THE FOUNDATIONS FOR BUILDING RESILIENCE

St. Eustace's was established in the late 1950s as a congregation governed under the same parish council as three others in the local community. In the mid-1990s, the four congregations became two, as smaller numbers prompted mergers. Like the experience of St. Jerome's in the last chapter, which included an amalgamation and changed leadership, St. Eustace's merged with one of the other two congregations and also gained a new priest around that time who began to encourage them to do more outreach in the community, prompting growth. In October of 2000, vandalism caused a fire to break out in St. Eustace's church building, damaging it beyond the point of being usable. After this, the congregation met in a school gym for four years while money was raised and plans were made for erecting a new church building. Shortly after moving into their new building, their priest retired and another new priest came who, again, reinvigorated the congregation to engage with the community around them. Around this time, some core members started an outreach program that involved planting community gardens and offering a free meal to community members once a week. They also began to open up their building to be used by other community organizations throughout the week to provide services like counseling, AA meetings, and English as a second language (ESL) instruction.

A further change was navigated when St. Eustace's became a congregation officially affirming of same-sex marriage and the LGBTQ2+ community. They inducted their most recent priest in 2015, whose ministry has produced further growth while still engaging the "Anglican core," as one participant suggested, referring to congregation members who had been there for thirty to forty years. Similar to experiences of leadership development and engaged laity at St. Jerome's in chapter two, the newest priest at St. Eustace is known for prioritizing the empowerment of members to lead through bringing them to courses on church growth and launching a center for spiritual renewal. As the center gained attention, new people continued to come from a variety of denominational backgrounds seeking the spiritual development and connection central to St. Eustace's flourishing. The congregation continued to grow until the COVID-19 pandemic presented St. Eustace's most recent challenge. When BC provincial health regulations around COVID-19 prevented in-person gatherings in 2020–21, the congregation pivoted and began providing online options for people to meet on Sundays and still participate in activities with the center for spiritual renewal. They continued to provide weekly meals to their community during this time in a take-out format. During the time of our case study work, St. Eustace's had recently begun meeting in person again on Sunday mornings while still providing an online option for attendance. Other ministries were also operating in hybrid form, and there was a sense among members that some families had yet to return and they were still in the process of understanding what it meant to be "re-flourishing" as a community.

CULTIVATING REPERTOIRES OF RESILIENCE AT ST. EUSTACE'S

Although presently engaged with how to emerge stronger out of the pandemic, St. Eustace's story as a congregation contains several turning points and challenges long before they faced the shared global challenge of COVID-19, and their response to these past events seems to have equipped them with a tool kit of resources for facing this most recent challenge. As we interviewed members, attended events, and observed the physical church building, we became interested in the optimistic way members shared about their past with us (and with one another) in relation to their present challenges around COVID-19 and the possible future of their parish.

Two aspirational narratives form part of this congregation's repertoire of resilience, each cultivated through seasons of challenge and change: (1) challenges, when faced collaboratively, make for an internally stronger, more innovative community; and (2) an openness to change through difficult transitions leads to growth, inclusion, and the capacity to face new challenges in the future.

Emerging from the Fire: Challenges Lead to Increased Internal Community Strength and Innovation

The first aspirational narrative cultivated in this congregation suggests that challenge, when faced together, creates internal community strength, resilience, and creativity. This narrative is encapsulated in the way congregation members talk about the fire, as with Drew, who said,

> A very present capacity in this congregation is . . . resilience. And so, when you look back at the history, you can see that resilience

is a particular trait. And because those are significant challenges, right—a fire and a merger and a movement into a [LGBTQ2+] inclusive congregation, launching a center for spiritual renewal—like those are not small things. So yeah, resilience is an apt description for this congregation.

The belief that a myriad of past challenges has led the congregation of St. Eustace's to become internally resilient is present in participant Katrina's quote. The strength of relationships and community connection at St. Eustace's were noted in all of our conversations and observations as one of this congregation's primary areas of flourishing. As we probed further, it became evident that this internal cohesion was at least partially cultivated by going "through trauma together," to use the current priest's words. This theme was especially strong when participants told stories about the fire that had burned down their previous church building in October of 2000. Coming out of this, the congregation did not have a building of their own for over four years. Congregants who were there during this time remember that the priest intentionally used this circumstance of being spiritually unhoused to start sharing in homilies and conversations a vision for what the church could be. As congregation member Darla remembers,

> She [the priest] started at that point talking about what does a church mean? . . . Is it the building that keeps us together? Is it the family that keeps us together? What is it? And that was huge.

In this in-between time, some leaders and members started studying a book called *Re-pitching the Tent* and having significant conversations over coffee, after church around tables in the gym, and during Bible studies where they began to innovatively reconceptualize what church could be and intentionally think about the design of the new church structure they would build.[10] Tasks like picking colors for the chairs and deciding on the layout of the building were facilitated by the priest in a collaborative way that "[brought] everyone closer," as Christopher said, noting that this "buys people in. The process buys people in, because I had a say. I might not have got exactly what I want, but I had a say." Going through this lengthy and difficult process collectively is generally perceived by the congregation to have strengthened community ties and ownership.

As a posture of optimism and process of collaborative innovation were promoted by the priest, members of St. Eustace's came to more positively

---

10. Giles, *Re-pitching the Tent*.

frame the impact of the fire on their overall identity and future prospects. As Christopher puts it, the narrative around the fire was as follows:

> This was not a tragedy. This was an opportunity. This was not "the congregation's dying." This was "the congregation's gonna flourish because what we can do out of this will be bigger and better than what we had before."

Beyond more casual storytelling among members, this narrative of emerging stronger from the fire is also ensconced in the St. Eustace's collective narrative in a few more official ways. First, their parish history document, written in narrative form, reflects this same optimistic approach to the fire and the four years spent setting up in a school gym that followed. It reads,

> As is often the case, adversity brought out the true mettle of the people. This time, often referred to by the congregation as "our journey in the wilderness," taught them that church is not about buildings but about people and also profoundly affected the design of the church they wanted to build.

Second, a significant symbol in St. Eustace's new building also serves as a more official reminder of this narrative of resilience: the charred cross from the old church, which hangs in a prominent place in the front of where they worship together every week (over the credence table where the communion elements are placed). This symbol acts as a tangible representation of their narrative of resilience and is even seen by some as connecting St. Eustace's to the broader narrative of the suffering and strength of the church throughout time. As Leigha said,

> That cross is originally from [the previous church building], and it's dark brown, and has a burnt look to it, because it went through the fire. And that's a symbol to me that I often look at thinking, yeah, the Church of all the ages, since the beginning of time has gone through difficult times, and yet he [Christ] lives and carries the power of that cross and what that cross symbolizes, you know, the resurrected new life of Christ for all people.

A Capacity for Change: Transitions Lead to Increased Growth, Inclusion, and Future Opportunity

"We do have a resilience, I think, of just being able to build, to build up when we need to pivot and when we need to change." As illustrated by Mary's words, the second tool in St. Eustace's repertoire of resilience is the overall openness they espouse as a community to transitions and change. From past mergers and leadership changes to becoming an LGBTQ2+ affirming community and developing significant new ministries, the congregation tells stories that suggest their openness to change has led to increased opportunities for growth and more inclusive engagement with the communities they serve.

This narrative thread is exemplified in how the church merger in the 1990s is talked about by parishioners who were there during that time. For these folks, it is looked back upon as a positive event which opened doors for future growth. As Drew said,

> For us at that time, it felt like a good move, because going from a congregation that was down [to] around thirty or so, joining another one of thirty. So, it felt like it was something that had some strength to it. And then that church started to grow.

The merger is just one of several examples of transitions brought up by interview participants that, while acknowledged as being sometimes difficult to navigate at the time, are reflected upon positively as ultimately opening doors to further growth and inclusion. Congregation members and leaders also talked about their transition to becoming a LGBTQ2+ affirming church and starting new ministries like community meals through a similar lens. Such transitions, members suggest, have led the congregation to be able to better actively serve marginalized groups in their parish and beyond and have created more space for growth within their congregation, as new people are drawn to their inclusive community.

It is important to note that an "openness to change," for St. Eustace parishioners, has not always meant that everyone agrees with the transitions taking place, or that change happens quickly. In their story, it has been important that decision making processes make room for dissenting voices and differences of opinion without compromising community belonging. Conversations around becoming an LGBTQ2+ affirming community, for example, were described by Dana as unfolding over "months and months and months and months," with some folks not being in support. But "did they stay with our church?" Dana continues, "They sure did." She attributed this to the process, which allowed their voices to be heard but not ultimately block the direction the broader community was going. Since that time, others have suggested that further reflection and being in closer proximity to members of the LGBTQ2+ community has caused several of the initial dissenters who stayed in the community to change their position. Chloe similarly suggests that, for the greater good and because of a strong trust in the leadership, even dissenting individuals in the congregation generally choose not to ultimately stymie change and can ultimately see its benefits further down the road.

> So, I think . . . an ethos of change has to happen to keep alive. And we might not always like where the change is going, but we're not going to go against it. And I think that's what keeps us moving forward.

St. Eustace's narratives surrounding times of past transition and change also impact the way they talk about future possibilities and present challenges. At the time of our interviews, the most pressing challenge was perceived to be reemerging as a flourishing community after the COVID-19 pandemic. Congregation members talked about the season of COVID restrictions as being very lonely and isolating for many, expressing concerns about when more members of the community still missing would come back to gather again. However, the overarching concern was not *if* they would reemerge as a stronger congregation but *how* and *when*. No serious doubts were expressed about the possibility of closure, financial hardship, or otherwise not making it through. Again, a narrative of optimism and resilience surrounded how parishioners and leaders talked about their future in light of pandemic challenges, drawing from their previous comebacks and capacity for change as evidence that they would make it through. As Christopher said,

> I think COVID has challenged us. And for some of us older Anglicans, I think it's scared us, you know? How are we going to come out the other end? And so, I think it raises a question mark . . . [but] we've re-pitched the tent once before, twice before. So, I think that in terms of that we can adjust, pivot. That's the word: pivot, and move forward.

CULTIVATING REPERTOIRES OF RESILIENCE IN YOUR CONGREGATION

Although past events were challenging, in telling the story of their church's history, members and leaders at St. Eustace's drew from cultivated repertoires of resilience that exist within their congregation—stories, symbols and ways of talking about the past that suggest hope for the future. While the content and context of the stories may differ, all congregations face times of challenge or transition. The concept of repertoires of resilience suggests that, even when challenges are out of a community's control, stories can still be meaningfully harnessed to influence how challenges are responded to. Any congregation can benefit from cultivating cultural repertoires of resilience to help frame challenges and changes in a way that might open pathways toward future flourishing. In learning from St. Eustace's story, we have identified three factors those who wish to cultivate repertoires of resilience might consider: (1) leader intentionality, (2) community trust and ownership, and (3) collaborative leadership.

First, St. Eustace's story teaches us that repertoires of resilience have a better chance of emerging when leaders or other key stakeholders in the community intentionally cultivate these repertoires, as such stories of hope and optimism in the midst of difficult circumstances seem unlikely to simply spring up on their own. In the example of emerging from the fire given above, the priest at the time laid the foundation for a story of resilience to emerge through her intentional framing of this event. She decided to talk about and actively teach on how the church could grow and become stronger from the fire and the opportunity it presented for them, as opposed to how it would shut them down or be their end. It thus seems that leaders or other key stakeholders in the community can have significant initial influence on how events and circumstances are perceived and responded to by the group; whether their response is intentional or not, it will likely influence perceived possibilities for the future.

As you consider your congregation, think about what types of stories are being told about where you have been and where you are going. Are they more optimistic or pessimistic? Who is shaping this culture, and does there seem to be an intentional desire to shape the narrative toward flourishing or in a different direction? Perhaps there has not been much intentionality around how past and present events are talked about, and people are choosing to see things through the lens of their own narratives.

Consider how you might use your leadership influence, however big or small it may seem, to offer a resilient perspective.

Second, repertoires of resilience mature and become solidified as part of the culture of organizations as members take ownership for telling and retelling these stories. This is seen in our case study in the way all congregation members we spoke to drew from similar, positive, common stocks of knowledge (stories) to describe the challenges and changes they had faced in the past. It became evident to us that the congregation as a whole had internalized these stories and symbols of resilience as part of their past, present, and future identity as a community. These were not just the stories of a few leaders anymore. In St. Eustice's story, the strong community belief and buy-in around these narratives seems to have been facilitated by trust both vertically (between parishioners and leaders) and horizontally (among parishioners). As Katrina said, "Trust, trust is really key. I think to why [St. Eustace's] has flourished, because there's trust." This trust is attributed to the continuity of some long-standing members who have gone through much life together, but it is also described as having been earned by each new priest (in part through vulnerability and humility), enabling them to have the currency, even among skeptical members, to lead into change.

As you think about laying the groundwork for repertoires of resilience to take root in your congregation, consider how you might encourage broader community buy-in ownership of the resilient narratives so they become part of the fabric of who you are as a church. Who are some other key community stakeholders who might be able to become early adaptors in championing the stories? What does trust look like right now among both congregation members toward one another and between congregants and leadership? If trust is strained, perhaps consider how it might be fostered first, as community buy-in may be more difficult to achieve in an environment of skepticism or mistrust.

Finally, St. Eustace's story teaches us that collaborative, as opposed to top-down, leadership approaches, seem to benefit the cultivation of repertoires of resilience toward flourishing within a community. This is in part because it encourages congregation members to take ownership of the cultural symbols and narratives of resilience, since they have a part in producing them. Collaboration, dialogue, and making room for opposing opinions were central to how stories around the fire and the congregation's identity as being open to change were solidified in St. Eustace's context.

There is the sense among the congregation that this is also a key for encouraging engagement overall in their community. As Katrina said,

> Yeah, I think that I do believe that [our current priest's] leadership style contributes in a significant way to what's happening at [St. Eustace's], in terms of his shared power approach. He's not dominating—it's not "power over." Because I feel like people take ownership then, right? They're like, "Hey, I have a part to play, I have something to contribute, and it's valued." And then people, you know, want to be involved.

A collaborative approach to change and decision making thus seems to lay the foundation for community involvement, meaning repertoires of resilience can emerge as meaningful cultural narratives with power and longevity.

As you reflect on your own context, consider what type of leadership approach tends to be taken in your congregation—more top-down or collaborative? How might more power and decision making be appropriately shared and others brought into the process as you seek to cultivate narratives of resilience? In your context, what would it look like for more collaborative decision making to be engaged so that everyone (even those with reservations) can be brought along on the journey and feel that they have a place to be heard?

CONCLUSION

In the context of St. Eustace's, we see how a history of hardship can be transformed into what we call *repertoires of resilience*, as opposed to repertoires of deficit or defeat. St. Eustace's history prompted us to consider how flourishing can be fostered in times of difficulty and disruption, not just when things seem to be going well. St. Eustace's teaches us that the aspirational narrative framing of past and present events is one strategy both leaders and congregation members can use to encourage resilience and open up pathways for positive action toward future flourishing.

QUESTIONS FOR REFLECTION

1. What types of stories are being told about where your congregation has been and where it is going? Who is shaping this culture, and

does the prevailing narrative lean toward flourishing or in a different direction?

2. What are the "repertoires of resilience" in your congregation that are aspirational and/or inspirational?

3. What does trust currently look like among congregation members toward one another and between congregants and leadership? How do these dynamics aid or hinder your congregation's ability to be resilient?

4. What type of leadership approach is taken in your congregation—top-down or collaborative? What would it look like for more collaborative decision making to be engaged so that everyone (even those with reservations) can be brought along on the journey and feel that they have a place to be heard?

BIBLIOGRAPHY

Boje, David M. "Stories of the Storytelling Organization: A Postmodern Analysis of Disney as 'Tamara-Land.'" *Academy of Management Journal* 38.4 (1995) 997–1035. https://doi.org/10.2307/256618.

Giles, R. *Re-pitching the Tent: Re-ordering the Church Building for Worship and Mission.* Norwich, UK: The Canterbury Press, 1996.

McAlpine, Bill, et al. *Signs of Life: Catholic, Mainline, and Conservative Protestant Congregations in Canada.* Toronto: Tyndale Academic, 2021.

Somers, Margaret. "Narrative and the Constitution of Identity: A Relational and Network Approach." *Theory and Society* 23 (1994) 605–49.

Swidler, A. "Culture in Action: Symbols and Strategies." *American Sociological Review*, 51.2 (1986) 273–86.

Yosso, T. J. "Whose Culture Has Capital? A Critical Race Theory Discussion of Community Cultural Wealth." *Race Ethnicity and Education*, 8.1 (2005) 69–91. https://doi.org/10.1080/1361332052000341006.

4

Flourishing in a Post-Christian Context
Two "Accessible" and "Relevant" Evangelical Churches in Quebec

Frédéric Dejean

LAUNCHING A CHURCH IN modern Quebec seems to be an activity with an unlikely chance of success. It would be similar to devoting all your energy to open and run a shop that only sells CDs, even though that market is decreasing from year to year. In Quebec, religious statistics—especially those regarding Christianity in its multiple offshoots—reveal an unprecedented crisis. For instance, more than 80 percent of Quebeckers declared themselves Catholics in 2001, declining to 75 percent in 2011 and 54 percent in 2021.[1] In reality, rather than new congregations being formed, we more often see closures, repurposing (into apartments, community centers, gyms), or even demolition of places of worship.

In this unfavorable climate to religious entrepreneurship, evangelical Protestant churches that portray themselves as "urban" have been launched by young "religion entrepreneurs." In this chapter, I will discuss two of them, La Chapelle and Axe21, which were studied from 2020 to 2023.[2] Ob-

---

1. Wilkins-Laflamme et al., "Indicateurs de religiosités."
2. For this research we used a qualitative approach: interviews with leaders (five to seven for each church) and members (fifteen for each church), participant observation during activities (meetings, house churches, and volunteering activities), and discourse analysis (Sunday messages and song lyrics).

viously, these two churches do not represent all facets of Quebec evangelical Protestantism. However, I propose approaching them as Christianity "laboratories" where the stories we'll hear reveal an offer—one believed to resonate with a secular post-Christian culture—that is developed and put to the religious market. In the following pages, I show that the two churches deploy multiple strategies stemming from an "accessibility theory" whose goal is to make the Church a "relevant" institution. That is to say, the central story in these congregations is that the content and medium that they provide is meaningful not only for their members, but also for the rest of society. In this way, one might liken "accessibility theory," and the desire to welcome all, to the "hospitable community" component of the Flourishing Congregations Construct in chapter one. "Accessibility theory" involves numerous points of contact between church culture and the culture in which individuals are immersed. To do this, I begin by contextualizing these two churches' stories within the Quebec religious landscape, then develop an "accessibility theory" that can be divided into several dimensions. Finally, I show how the two churches make relevance the goal of this accessibility quest. Although different from St. Jerome's parish in chapter two, the two congregations in this chapter reveal once more the important role that innovation plays in churches that seem to flourish in the face of transition and change.

LA CHAPELLE AND AXE21 IN QUEBEC'S EVANGELICAL LANDSCAPE

The Recent Deep Transformation of the Religious Landscape in Quebec

Quebec has deep Catholic roots, especially from the second half of the nineteenth century until the Quiet Revolution.[3] This revolution was a period of rapid and deep transformation: industrialization, urbanization, and, at a religious level, a secularization process epitomized by the plummeting attendance experienced by the Catholic Church and Protestant mainstream denominations since.

Parallel to these declines, evangelicals in Quebec experienced a phase of "Awakening" during the 1970s and 1980s.[4] For instance, Rich-

---

3. Zubrzycki, *Beheading the Saint*.
4. Di Giacomo, "Religious Entrepreneurship"; Lougheed, "Evangelical Revivals";

ard Lougheed observed that the number of congregations of four major denominations (Plymouth Brethren, Fellowship Baptist, Baptist Union, and Mennonite Brethren) in French Canada grew steadily from the 1960s onward: 42 in 1960, 53 in 1970, 101 in 1980, and 141 in 1990.[5] Today, they benefit from three concurrent phenomena: (1) significant growth in immigrant churches—Haitian, African and Latin American—mainly located in the Montreal metropolitan area; (2) a missionary effort originating in English-speaking Canada or the USA; and finally, (3) Francophone "religion entrepreneurship," primarily anchored in the Baptist tradition, which is developing a renewed and innovative religious option, mainly inspired by churches in the USA. Although it is modest,[6] this positive dynamic is quite remarkable when compared to the profound crisis the Catholic Church[7] and mainstream Protestant denominations are experiencing.[8] The most recent data released by Statistics Canada in 2021 showed that in Quebec, evangelical groups were the only Christian tradition to maintain their proportionate hold of the population, even increasing slightly. Between 1971 and 2021, the proportion of Quebeckers affiliated to a "conservative protestant" church rose from 0.9 percent to around 1.5 percent of the population.[9]

La Chapelle and Axe21: Two Nondenominational Churches Breaking with Tradition

La Chapelle and Axe21 are two churches that launched recently (2010 and 2013, respectively). They are based on Baptist theology and led by pastors in their forties (members of pastoral teams in each church range from twenty-five to forty years old). Both churches are distinctive in that they are multi-site churches.[10] Prior to the COVID-19 pandemic, La Chapelle held gatherings in three locations in Montreal (a theater and two school

---

Lougheed et al., *Protestantisme au Québec*; Smith, "French Speaking Protestantism."

5. Lougheed, "Evangelical Revivals," 200–201.

6. According to Statistics Canada's 2021 National Household Survey, approximately 75 percent of Quebeckers identified themselves as Christians. Almost 54 percent of Quebeckers were Catholics. Protestant traditions were therefore in the minority: 0.4 percent were Baptists, 0.5 percent were Pentecostals, and 0.2 percent were in the United Church.

7. Meunier and Wilkins-Laflamme, "Sécularisation, catholicisme et transformation."

8. Wilkins-Laflamme et al., "Indicateurs de Religiosités."

9. Wilkins-Laflamme et al., "Indicateurs de Religiosités."

10. Bird et al., *Multi-site Church Revolution*.

auditoriums). In 2021, the church began two assemblies outside Montreal: one in Gatineau and the other in Quebec City (La Chapelle Québec). After only one year, over six hundred adults attended one of two Sunday morning services at La Chapelle Québec. The youth leader explained that often over one hundred children attend Sunday school.[11] Axe21 meets in two midsize cities in the Eastern Townships (Sherbrooke and Magog). In 2016, the church acquired the municipal theater located on Magog's main street. Other than church activities, the theater hosts nonreligious programs that traditionally take place in this type of building (for instance, concerts, plays, or stand-up comedy shows). In the context of Quebec, these multisite churches show a sense of innovation, in that these two churches are open to and experimenting with new ideas. The pastors who launched the two churches fall into the category of "religion entrepreneurs" as described by Richard N. Pitt. Pitt points out that "entrepreneurship is a process of recognizing an opportunity to create new goods or services (or ways to deliver them) and then acting on this recognition."[12] Religious entrepreneurship includes three elements: identifying a business opportunity, designing and developing goods and services, and implementing distribution strategies that best represent the offer and demand in a given context.

The first element—identifying opportunities—is critical because the success of subsequent operations depends on it. For the founders of Axe21 and La Chapelle, the effort to launch new congregations resulted from the realization of a growing gap between the existing Christian offerings and modern Quebec culture, dominated by values such as individualism, rejection of strong institutional constraints, and aspirations for "authenticity."[13] This has an impact on church members who have difficulty reconciling their daily lives with life in the church but also on "seekers" who cannot find a religious offering in line with their desires (friendliness, teachings useful for daily life, or social involvement in the community). The founding pastors of the two churches began from the premise—the story or narrative, if you will—that most churches operate as "clubs" focused solely on their members and are therefore unable to catch the attention of people who are less familiar with Christianity. Before we hear from one interviewee,

---

11. During the summer of 2023, La Chapelle Québec (The Chapel Quebec) changed its name and is now called Nouvelle Vie Québec (New Life Quebec). This new name indicates that on an institutional level, the church has joined the megachurch Nouvelle Vie (New Life) located in a Montreal suburb.

12. Pitt, *Church Planters*, 4.

13. Taylor, *Malaise of Modernity*, 25.

it is worth considering, what are the starting or guiding assumptions that inform your church's approach to ministry, both with those inside and outside your congregation? In your estimation, how (un)helpful are those premises for including or excluding different groups? Drawing once more on the Flourishing Congregations Construct, naming these frameworks can help a church to articulate the healthy and not-so-healthy aspects to congregational self-identity and culture.

In an interview, one of the founders of Axe21 recounted an experience that opened his eyes:

> I had brought seven of my friends from college to the Baptist church.... So, we arrived on Sunday morning, then entered the room, and in many evangelical churches there are large neon lights, the room is bright, then you come in, and my friends felt like they were kind of in the spotlight.... All of a sudden, everyone stood up and started singing. My friends were shocked because they had never seen that in their life. Just the fact that people would stand up together and sing—culturally in Quebec we don't do that except for the national anthem at the Bell Centre. ... Also, from the first song, the words were completely disconnected from something they could understand—something like, "We cast our crowns before the Lamb on the throne" or "For He is the Lamb that was slain." ... After only 5 minutes, my friends were convinced they were in a cult.[14]

The experience described by this pastor convinced him that it was vital to ensure that the church takes on a form that resonates with the general cultural system Quebeckers experience. Defined as a "set of publicly shared codes or repertoires, building blocks that structure people's ability to think and to share ideas,"[15] culture carries a grammar of thought and patterns of action that serve as resources available to individuals. Regarding religion, these resources have an impact on "plausibility structures,"[16] or a group's taken-for-granted worldviews, which are closely linked to a given culture. Since 1967, Peter Berger has emphasized that "as there is a secularization of society and culture, so is there a secularization of consciousness."[17] Philosopher Charles Taylor underscored the effects of "secularity" on conditions of possibility of religious belief when he discussed "conditions of belief": "The

---

14. All French quotations in this text have been rendered in English by the author.
15. Eliasoph and Lichterman, "Culture in Interaction," 735.
16. Berger, *Sacred Canopy*, 47.
17. Berger, *Sacred Canopy*, 167.

shift to secularity in this sense consists, among other things, of a move from a society where belief in God is unchallenged and indeed, unproblematic, to one in which it is understood to be one option among others, and frequently not the easiest to embrace."[18] Practically then, Axe21 leaders work with the narrative that they cannot afford to neglect discussion—even if it takes the form of radical rejection—with the culture its members come from.

While leaders of the two churches recognize there is tension between dominant norms and values in Quebec society and those their churches hold, the fact remains that this tension must be part of a dialogue in such a way that the church does not simply lose the attention of its contemporaries. La Chapelle and Axe21 focus their congregational identity and narrative on the goal of being accessible to outsiders to bring together the Quebec culture with the culture of the church. The challenge for leaders is therefore to speak the language of Quebec culture to disseminate their message in the channels that shape that culture. In the next section, I show how the two churches seek to make church culture compatible with the culture in which individuals find themselves, through mobilizing what I call an "accessibility theory."

AVOIDING "SELECTIVE BAFFLES": AN ACCESSIBILITY THEORY

Churches That Are Compatible with Culture

Like many other nondenominational Christian congregations, La Chapelle and Axe21 make accessibility a central objective on many levels: theological, ritual, cultural, and even spatial. This accessibility focuses on creating a continuum between individuals' daily lives and what they can experience within the church, so that these do not appear to be two separate worlds. On this point, the evangelical world is quite inconsistent. Some churches stress tension with and perhaps even separation from their environment as a powerful driver of their action. This attitude is expressed by "sheltered enclave theory."[19] According to this theory, it is essential to create real or symbolic barriers between the group and the rest of society, because secular culture—controlled by pluralism, individualism, relativism, or instrumental

---

18. Taylor, *Secular Age*, 3.
19. Smith and Emerson, *American Evangelicalism*, 67.

rationality—is basically a threat to the group's integrity. La Chapelle and Axe21 completely oppose this attitude since they implement mechanisms that leave no "incompatibilities" between what is experienced within and outside the church. To denote these, I have borrowed semiologist Roland Barthes's expression of "selective baffles," used in his essay "The Pleasure of Text." Describing literature, Barthes writes that "the text is a fetish, and this fetish desires me. The text chooses me, by a whole disposition of invisible screens, selective baffles: vocabulary, references, readability, etc."[20] Unlike a wall that does not differentiate and simply blocks anyone from entering, the "baffle" allows for distinguishing between people who know the codes for understanding the text and others.

In the religious sphere, "selective baffles" can take the form of discursive content (canonical or sacred texts but also discourses produced by clerics, who must have the keys of understanding to grasp the meaning of such texts), rituals (particularly those that involve the body and handling objects), and space-time enshrined in buildings. Some research on evangelicalism highlights its ability to be accessible to as many people as possible, regardless of their cultural and religious background. In that respect, anthropologist Thomas Csordas, reflecting on "what travels well across geographical and cultural space," identified "two aspects of religions that must be attended to in determining whether or not they travel well, what I will call portable practice and transposable message." He elaborates,

> By portable practice I mean rites that can be easily learned, require relatively little esoteric knowledge or paraphernalia, are not held as proprietary or necessarily linked to a specific cultural context, and can be performed without commitment to an elaborate ideological or institutional apparatus. . . . By transposable message I mean that the basis of appeal contained in religious tenets, premises, or promises can find footing across a diversity of linguistic and cultural settings.[21]

Whether "portable practice" or "transposable message," the central quality highlighted is accessibility of content and practices, whose simplicity and likelihood of resonating with various cultural contexts contribute to their success on a global scale. More broadly, accessibility is an essential trait in the analysis of some streams of evangelicalism in terms of democratization of the religious experience. As historian Nathan Hatch, who

---

20. Barthes, *Pleasure of the Text*, 27.
21. Csordas, "Introduction," 260–61.

analyzed the emergence of Baptists and Methodists in the United States in the wake of the U.S. War of Independence, describes, "These religious activists pitched their message to the unschooled and unsophisticated. Their movements offered the humble a marvelous sense of individual potential and collective aspiration."[22] While some expressions of modern evangelicalism in Quebec go beyond the "unschooled and unsophisticated," the fact remains that the two churches strive to make possible an authentic religious experience that fits with the ethos of what Galen Watts defines a "romantic liberal modernity,"[23] an alternative to a rational liberalism. To speak of liberal Romanticism is to insist on the importance of emotion and individual quest for authenticity as the driving cultural force in contemporary Western democracies.

Without inferring that your church ought to be compatible in form or content with the wider culture, it is valuable to identify the ways that your church's posture to society aids or hinders your group's ability to flourish. In this regard, what does or would it mean for your congregation to flourish on theological, sociological, or ecclesiological terms?

Religious Metalanguage

It is November 2021 and the Sherbrooke Axe21 church is currently holding gatherings in Bishop University's concert hall. This Sunday morning, ten people will be baptized. At the beginning of the service, the youth pastor comes to center stage and begins to speak.

> For you, this morning might be your first time at Axe21, and I would like to especially welcome you. You consider yourself a skeptic. Maybe you are curious about God, so I would like to explain a bit to you about what this church is like. This is a church that meets at Bishop, but seriously, we could meet anywhere, because the most important message for us is the message of the Bible. We believe in Jesus Christ, we believe in the truth that the Bible expresses to us, but we believe that the church must still be relevant for us today. That's why you are going to see that our pastor wears regular clothes. As for me, sometimes I wish he had a robe just because it would be funny. . . . If you're wondering who I am, besides the guy who's in front this morning, my name is Corentin and I am the youth leader here at Axe21. What is a youth leader,

---

22. Hatch, *Democratization*, 5.
23. Watts, *Spiritual Turn*, 61.

besides making announcements now and then? Well, I take care of teens.... Before handing this over to Pastor Jasmin, I will explain what we are currently doing at Axe: we have a theme called faith and rationality. I love this theme, because we are trying to show that faith and rationality sometimes go together, but other times you just have to take a step of faith. That's what we're going to look at this morning with Jasmin before the baptisms.[24]

While the pastor's words are motivated by the fact that on baptism days, people who are not Christian or are unfamiliar with the evangelical sphere are likely to be present, this type of public discourse is common. Borrowing a term that originated in linguistics,[25] I am speaking of "religious metalanguage" to refer to the fact that during a religious activity, someone explains the religious activity in a way that helps members of congregations and visitors who are not necessarily familiar with it to understand its meaning. The excerpt quoted above illustrates that this religious metalanguage covers several dimensions: the identity of the church and its theological setting—"We believe in Jesus Christ, we believe in the truth that the Bible expresses to us, but we believe that the Church must still be relevant for us today"; positions held by leaders—"I am the youth leader here at Axe21. What is a youth leader[?] . . . Well, I take care of teens"; the meaning of the current activity—"We are trying to show that faith and rationality sometimes go together, but other times you just have to take a step of faith." Religious metalanguage explains the church's activities more so than its beliefs to an audience of people unfamiliar with Christian life or how evangelical congregations operate. That is, during Sunday morning gatherings, pastors explain what they are doing and why they do it.

Here too, in your context it could be worthwhile to consider how you include or exclude certain groups based on the absence of religious metalanguage that could make some components of your collective gatherings inaccessible to some people. If including religious metalanguage is not a priority in your church—for which there may be good theological or sociological reasons—are there other ways that those less familiar with your tradition might come to learn and understand the group's practices and

---

24. Jasmin is the pastor of Sherbrooke Axe21.

25. "When a speaker does not use language to speak of people (of others, etc.), but rather to speak of language or expression (both written and verbal), we say the speaker is carrying out a metalinguistic activity (or related to metalanguage), meaning the language (or the expression) itself becomes the subject of study or speaking." Reuter et al., "Métalangage," 123.

rituals, so that they can follow along and meaningfully experience what insiders have come to value in your congregation? These questions once more call attention to what it means for congregations to be hospitable communities as part of their flourishing.

Toward a "Safe Religious Space"

The function of religious metalanguage is to explain—somewhat like subtitles in the original version of a movie—but also to reassure people who have questions about the activity they are participating in. Therefore, all efforts are made to create a feeling of comfort and to provide access to "an authentic encounter" with Jesus. In this regard, one of the Axe21 pastors explained in an interview,

> We are aware there is a shocking message in the Bible. If you feel stuck in trying to come to God because of that message, that doesn't bother me. However, if you feel stuck because of all the obstacles around you, for example, decor, musical style, the way I present myself, the way I talk to you, or my language, that makes me sad. Here, we are trying to remove everything that blocks access to the core message.

Another Axe21 pastor expressed a similar viewpoint:

> I told myself that when we started Axe21, I wanted the only obstacle to be the cross, as the gospel message. Because my friends have not refused the gospel message. They have refused an institution, a way of doing things; they have rejected the wrapping paper, not the gift. They found the wrapping paper so ugly, if you will, that they did not even wait around to see the gift inside.

A pastor at La Chapelle Québec followed this same line of thought during a Sunday morning discussion before the worship service started. "We have created an 'experience team' that specifically ensures that the experience here is the best possible. In this way, if they are not touched, it is not because of something we could have taken action on."

The two churches expend considerable effort to create a space where people feel comfortable. This is what I call a "religious safe space."[26] By

---

26. The idea of "safe space" emerged in the last decades of the twentieth century within feminist movements (see Roestone Collective, "Safe Space"). It involved women having places and times to meet as women and thus safely share their concerns, without fearing masculine scrutiny. Later, this idea was extended to groups of people who suffer

this expression, I identify a mechanism that is both spatial and temporal that promotes inclusion of each participant, regardless of religious background or spiritual progress. It primarily involves making everyone feel comfortable. As one Axe21 pastor mentioned,

> We want our welcome process to represent very good customer service, but no more. We don't want it to be intrusive. We don't want people coming through the door of the church to be asked too many questions—"Are you new here? Have you already given your life to the LORD? Have you been born again?"—or things like that.

Creating such a religious safe space requires concern for detail and attention to things that may seem trivial but prove to be vital as soon as other people mention them. For example, Axe21 and La Chapelle make a point of serving quality coffee. "Most churches serve cheap coffee; we want to serve good coffee here," confided one pastor. Besides the enjoyment it provides, coffee serves a very specific function for people who are alone. One Axe21 pastor emphasized this point: "Often when someone is alone, even more when they are in an unfamiliar place, they don't know how to act or move; having a coffee in their hands, that gives them some composure. It's reassuring."

As the expression "religious safe space" suggests, places where churches meet are not randomly chosen. While we must remember church plants contend with strong constraints with little latitude regarding the places they meet, these urban church leaders spend time reflecting on places where members meet. One of the Axe21 founders testified to this:

> What obstacle prevents people from hearing the Bible message? We came to the conclusion that . . . the place we meet is intimidating. It's a church, which is kind of off-putting for most people. It's not always very welcoming. . . . This led to our decision to rent the Granada Theatre, which is the oldest theater in Sherbrooke and that everyone knows about. Everyone comes here for one reason or other. So, it's a neutral place where everyone has gone and knows where the entrance and exit are. They don't have to worry about being trapped here; you enter easily and leave whenever you want.

---

forms of domination and oppression.

Removing Rituality

In our Flourishing Congregations Construct, we highlighted that a hospitable community is an important dimension to congregational flourishing. At La Chapelle and Axe21, special attention is devoted to the quality of community life. It is also frequently mentioned that the church is not a place or a building but a community of people who want to share a life of faith. As one pastor emphasized on a Sunday, "the Church is not a building, it's the people who gather inside it." For an individual, experiencing church is therefore experiencing a collaborative group with whom the same faith is shared. Preferred times for this experience are Sunday morning "gatherings" or "meetings" whose distinctive feature is their simplicity of form, with a three-part structure: music (about twenty minutes); message (thirty to thirty-five minutes); and music (about fifteen minutes). Meetings begin with a welcome where one of the leaders mainly addresses people who have come for the first time. During one of my visits to the Mile End La Chapelle (Montreal), the pastor responsible for the welcome invited people who were there for the first time to collect their "gift bag," which included a shopping bag bearing the church logo, a Bible, and a mug that had the logo and an inspirational saying.

The formal simplicity of meetings is a key element in accessibility and echoes "portable practices" that do not require ceremonial objects, specific spatial mechanisms, or particular knowledge.[27] This is what is striking when participating in a meeting at one of the two churches: church rituals take on familiar cultural forms. While there are, of course, consistent sequences that punctuate the meetings, they draw upon what is familiar from pop music concerts and TED conferences. Such simplicity serves a few functions. First, this formal simplicity allows those who come for the first time to not feel lost or out of sync with the rest of the congregation. Not knowing what to do and when to do it could create a feeling of embarrassment and exclusion. Second, simplicity leaves the door open to multiple ways of experiencing "meetings." During singing segments alternating between praise songs with upbeat rhythms and soft and meditative worship songs, the posture of those within the congregation is diverse. Some are standing, moving to the rhythm of the music and lifting their hands; in contrast, others stay still with their eyes closed. One member of La Chapelle thus explained in an interview: "I love the ambiance in the room on Sundays.

---

27. Csordas, "Introduction," 261.

With subdued lighting and semi-darkness, I feel I can experience the meeting my own way, without feeling obligated to adopt specific postures and ways of acting." This quote reminds us that even if places do not determine action, they offer possibilities and opportunities for action. In this sense, they are material elements that interact with practical dispositions.[28] In this case, the specific features of a theater make possible or impossible some behaviors. For instance, it is easy to worship standing up, whereas it is hard to do so on one's knees.

The efforts manifested by La Chapelle and Axe21 to make themselves accessible to as many people as possible and to establish consistent and fruitful dialogue between church life and the rest of society are part of a larger project by pastoral teams to be "relevant" congregations. Aside from the initial rapid growth and sustained size since, it is difficult to fully assess whether these storylines and practices related to relevance resonate with most in these congregations, notably those visiting for the first time. Interviews and surveys with congregants on these points would be helpful. What is important for our purposes in this book is to highlight the narratives that congregations tell themselves and others to navigate transition and change, which in these church contexts involve mass social and religious change external to the local church that have implications for how congregations seek to minister. The next section offers a window into how Axe21 and La Chapelle tell their story of relevance in a broadly secular Quebec context.

AXE21 AND LA CHAPELLE: TWO RELEVANT CHURCHES IN QUEBEC

What Does It Mean to Be "Relevant" from an Evangelical Perspective?

During an interview, one pastor of Axe21 explained that "every meeting starts with a short presentation of who we are and what we do at Axe21. It's a way to welcome newcomers. We explain that we're a normal church and that we want the church to be more accessible to people who want to experience the Christian faith. We emphasize that Axe21 is a church relevant to twenty-first-century Quebec." Later in the same interview, talking about the consequences of the COVID-19 pandemic on church activities, especially the shift from in-person activities to online activities, he shared his

---

28. Bourdieu, *Sens pratique*.

perceptions that "when we started to make our message available online, I realized that it was not attractive to non-Christian people. That's why in April 2020 we held a very important meeting, during which I told the other pastors we would have to work hard if we wanted to be relevant online for non-Christian people."[29] A pastor of La Chapelle shared a similar perspective: "So, our main objective is to help people experience an authentic encounter with Jesus but in a way which is relevant and useful in their lives." These remarks demonstrate that "relevance" is a value and narrative that directs the actions of the two churches.

What does "relevance" or "relevant church" mean? *The Oxford Dictionary* gives two short definitions of relevance: "(1) a close connection with the subject you are discussing or the situation you are in; and (2) being valuable and useful to people in their lives and work."[30] These two definitions complement each other. According to the second definition, "relevance" is synonymous with "usefulness." The first definition of relevance invites us to deepen the idea of a "close connection" between a person and a situation they must deal with. A relevant church is not only an institution that meets spiritual and emotional needs, and sometimes social and material needs, but it is more deeply an institution directly connected to the cultural context in which it is embedded, as suggested in interviews with church leaders.

This close link between a church and the culture is at the core of some key texts that mobilize the idea of relevance. For example, this is the case with *Center Church*, a renowned handbook by Timothy Keller, which was translated into French in 2015. Drawing on terminology created by sociologist James Davison Hunter,[31] Keller uses the word "relevance" when he introduces a typology of four models of how evangelicals relate to culture: (1) the "transformationist model"; (2) "the relevance model"; (3) the "counterculturalist model"; and (4) the "two Kingdoms model."[32] The "relevance model" sketched out by Keller is reminiscent of models developed by Niebuhr,[33] especially the latter's second model ("Christ of culture") and third model ("Christ above culture"), which is the most positive regarding culture. Keller asserts that:

---

29. Note, such perceptions are difficult to independently verify.
30. *Oxford Learner's Dictionary*, s.v. "Relevance."
31. Hunter, *Change the World*.
32. Keller, *Center Church*, 194.
33. Niebuhr, *Christ and Culture*.

> The animating idea behind these approaches is that God's Spirit is at work in the culture to further his Kingdom; therefore Christians should view culture as their ally and join with God to do good.... The primary way to engage culture, then, is for the church to adapt to new realities and connect to what God is doing in the world.[34]

Churches that hold this paradigm have several characteristics in common: they are sympathetic to cultural developments; pay special attention to the common good; and make the church a tool for justice. Ultimately,

> relevants seek to engage culture by reinventing the church's ministry to be more relevant to the needs and sensibilities of people in the culture and more committed to the service and good of the whole human community. While not condoning immorality and relativism, they locate the main problem in the church's incomprehensibility to the minds and hearts of secular people and its irrelevance to the problems of society.[35]

How to Be a "Relevant" Church in Quebec

In Hunter's words, churches "in the 'relevance to' paradigm make a priority of being connected to the pressing issues of the day.... Their emphasis is less on the defense of the faith than on being relevant and connected to contemporary culture."[36] This remark perfectly applies to the two churches under study here: their focus is primarily on their ability to enter into dialogue and resonate with modern Quebec culture, while theological content directly coming from evangelical faith is not very evident, at least not in the communications sent out by the two churches. The following image shows a banner photographed at La Chapelle Québec, and the same image appears in other locations of La Chapelle and on the church website. It reads, "A relevant church, young in spirit, inclusive, creative, and generous. A church that challenges perceptions and restores the image of Christianity in society. A church focused on the message of hope and love of Jesus Christ. A Church that loves God, that loves people, that love the city. A church that accompanies people on their spiritual journey and equips them in all areas of their lives, so that they in turn influence the lives of others."

---

34. Keller, *Center Church*, 200.
35. Keller, *Center Church*, 202.
36. Hunter, *To Change the World*, 215–16.

Banner at the entrance of La Chapelle Québec (FD, October 2022)

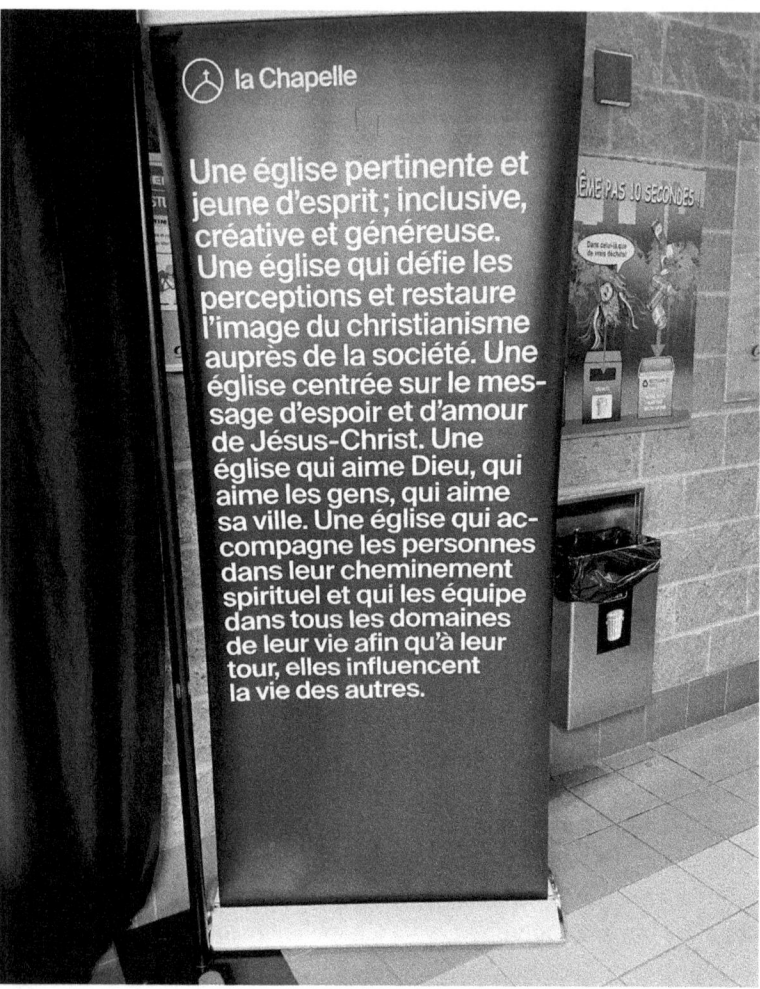

This is a form of a "profession of faith" that begins with the affirmation that the church is "relevant." This approach differentiates La Chapelle from what they assume is traditionally seen in other evangelical churches, which usually involves the affirmation of the need for Christians to acknowledge their sinful state and their salvation in Christ. Furthermore, the close connection between Quebec society and church life is clearly affirmed: La Chapelle aims to "reestablish the image of Christianity in the view of society," an affirmation that acknowledges the fact that sexual and financial scandals or the painful legacy of Indigenous residential schools have contributed significantly to the deterioration of Quebeckers' perception of Christianity. In this framing, we see parallels to efforts in some other evangelical congregations to redeem a "spoiled identity."[37] In addition, we find in this affirmation the idea that the church is not an institution designed to only serve its members but is more generally designed for everyone ("a church ... that loves people and loves its city").

Opening the church up to the rest of society, and being committed to people in general, especially those most vulnerable, are critical aspects in this quest for relevance. Reflective of the "outward dimension" of the Flourishing Congregations Construct, during interviews with members from the two congregations, it was evident that one of the most appreciated aspects was a commitment to serve the community. La Chapelle created a community organization independent of the church, whose name, J'aime ma ville (I love my city), well illustrates the church's integration in its urban environment. While J'aime ma ville offers services, such as a food bank for low-income households (being a member of the church is not required to benefit from this) and a mentoring system for newly arrived immigrants in Quebec, its distinctiveness is that it supports the action of community organizations by periodically offering volunteers, most of whom are members of La Chapelle. The image below shows one of these activities in which I participated, when about ten J'aime ma ville volunteers prepared packets containing salad dressing.

The defining feature of these activities is that they are done in a spirit of service and not for the goal of proselytizing. In interviews, leaders from the two churches emphasized that aspect: the goal of service activities is not to recruit members or convert people. Furthermore, volunteers who participate are reminded that their mission is specifically to serve and not to evangelize. If there is a form of evangelism, it is through the dimension of the witness that their service embodies. This approach is consistent with Canadian-based research that suggests an apprehension to overt evangelism.[38] The assumption is that evangelism is too offensive to a secular audience, with Canadians presumably sensitive and resistant to Christianity's colonial legacy with its local and global missionary and proselytization efforts.

---

37. Schuurman, *Subversive Evangelical*, 7.
38. Thiessen et al., "Evangelistic Belief."

Volunteer activity at Mission Bon Accueil in Montreal organized by J'aime ma ville (FD, June 2022)

CONCLUSION

While La Chapelle and Axe21 do not convey all the complexity of the Quebec evangelical landscape, they do represent two excellent "laboratories" of Christianity in the context of a post-Christian society. Even though Quebec, a city where until recently Catholicism played a prominent social and cultural role, seems to have mainly turned away from Christianity, the two churches demonstrate possibility, presence, and "flourishing" in an environment that at first glance seems unsupportive of them. In this chapter, I have shown that the implementation of "accessibility theory" results in the creation of a continuum between Quebec culture and church subculture, thereby breaking away from the idea that the identity of a church is based on a gap between it and the rest of society. Furthermore, all the methods employed to ensure this accessibility contribute more broadly to a vision held by the two churches, which is built around the idea of "relevance." This upholds the double calling of the two congregations: to be sensitive to daily challenges faced by their members and to needs of the broader society to which they are fully committed.

Recalling from chapter one that congregational culture is impacted by several factors that include what is occurring in the wider society, Axe21 and La Chapelle remind us that the stories congregations tell operate within a larger cultural system and set of assumptions both internal and external to a local church. To think or practice otherwise is problematic for congregational flourishing. Similar to St. Jerome's in chapter two, the congregations featured in this chapter took bold and innovative steps that reflect a clear self-identity, targeted messaging along with systems and structures, and a hospitable community. Simply because these dynamics exist does not mean that a congregation will flourish. But these qualities appear to be important facets of flourishing in the Quebec context, mindful again of the dynamic and unique interplay of factors that any single congregation faces.

QUESTIONS FOR REFLECTION

1. What do you think are the central aims of the local church? In what ways does your church embody (or not) these purposes?
2. How, if at all, do you think your congregation could or should minister within a changing Canadian social context?
3. What practices in your congregation are "accessible" or "inaccessible" to people who are not familiar with the Christian culture?

BIBLIOGRAPHY

Barthes, Roland. *The Pleasure of the Text*. New York: Hill and Wang, 2009.
Berger, Peter L. *The Sacred Canopy: Elements of a Sociological Theory of Religion*. New York: Anchor Books, 1967.
Bird, Warren, et al. *The Multi-site Church Revolution: Being One Church in Many Locations*. Grand Rapids: Zondervan, 2009.
Bourdieu, Pierre. *Le sens pratique*. Paris: Éditions de Minuit, 1980.
Csordas, Thomas J. "Introduction: Modalities of Transnational Transcendence." *Anthropological Theory* 7.3 (Sept. 1, 2007) 259–72.
Di Giacomo, Michael. "Religious Entrepreneurship in Quebec in the 1970s and 1980s." *Journal of the Canadian Church Historical Society* 46.1 (2004) 49–88.
Eliasoph, Nina, and Paul Lichterman. "Culture in Interaction." *American Journal of Sociology* 108.4 (Jan. 1, 2003) 735–94.

Hatch, Nathan O. *The Democratization of American Christianity*. New Haven: Yale University Press, 1989.

Hunter, James Davison. *To Change the World: The Irony, Tragedy, and Possibility of Christianity in the Late Modern World*. New York: Oxford University Press, 2010.

Keller, Timothy. *Center Church: Doing Balanced, Gospel-Centered Ministry in Your City*. Grand Rapids: Zondervan, 2012.

Lougheed, Richard. "The Evangelical Revivals of the 1960s-80s." In *French Speaking Protestantism in Canada*, 191–206. Leiden: Brill, 2011.

Lougheed, Richard, et al. *Histoire du Protestantisme au Québec depuis 1960: Une analyse anthropologique, culturelle et historique*. Collection Sentier. Québec: Éd. La Clairière, 1999.

Meunier, É-Martin, and Sarah Wilkins-Laflamme. "Sécularisation, catholicisme et transformation du régime de religiosité au Québec: Étude comparative avec le catholicisme au Canada (1968-2007); Catholicisme et laïcité au Québec." *Recherches Sociographiques* 52.3 (2011) 683–729.

Niebuhr, H. Richard. *Christ and Culture*. San Francisco: Harper, 2001.

Pitt, Richard N. *Church Planters: Inside the World of Religion Entrepreneurs*. New York: Oxford University Press, 2022.

Reuter, Yves, et al. "Métalangage—activité métalinguistique." In *Dictionnaire des concepts fondamentaux des didactiques*, 3:123–28. Hors Collection. Louvain-la-Neuve, BE: De Boeck Supérieur, 2013.

The Roestone Collective. "Safe Space: Towards a Reconceptualization." *Antipode* 46.5 (2014) 1346–65.

Schuurman, Peter. *The Subversive Evangelical: The Ironic Charisma of an Irreligious Megachurch*. Advancing Studies in Religion 6. Montreal: McGill-Queen's University Press, 2019.

Smith, Christian, and Michael Emerson. *American Evangelicalism: Embattled and Thriving*. Chicago: University of Chicago Press, 1998.

Smith, Glenn. "A Brief Socio-demographic Portrait of French Speaking Protestantism in Quebec since 1960." In *French-Speaking Protestants in Canada: Historical Essays*, 265–83. Leiden: Brill, 2011.

Taylor, Charles. *The Malaise of Modernity*. Concord, ON: Anansi, 2003.

———. *A Secular Age*. Cambridge: Harvard University Press, 2007.

Thiessen, Joel, et al. "Evangelistic Belief and Behaviour among Canadian Congregants." *Studies in Religion* 51 (2021) 459–79.

Watts, Galen. *The Spiritual Turn: The Religion of the Heart and the Making of Romantic Liberal Modernity*. New York: Oxford University Press, 2022.

Wilkins-Laflamme, Sarah, et al. "L'évolution des indicateurs de religiosités dans les traditions Chrétiennes de la province du Québec: Cinq décennies de déclins, d'essor et de diversification." In *Étudier les Christianismes dans un contexte de post-Chrétienté*, edited by Frédéric Dejean and Catherine Foisy. Sainte-Foy: Presses de l'Université Laval, forthcoming.

Zubrzycki, Geneviève. *Beheading the Saint: Nationalism, Religion, and Secularism in Quebec*. Chicago: University of Chicago Press, 2016.

5

Stories of Spiritual Formation and Growth at St. John's Anglican Church
The Importance of Social Ties

Arch Chee Keen Wong

INTRODUCTION

WHAT IS THE FUNCTION of stories or narratives for a flourishing congregation? James Hopewell suggests that "storyline expresses the intricacy of congregational life. Though widely regarded as merely a form of entertainment or illustration, stories are an essential account of social experience."[1] For Hopewell, there are at least two fundamental relationships between congregational life and stories: (1) a congregation's self-understanding of itself happens primarily through narrative; and (2) a congregation's way of communication among its members happens mainly by storyline. The stories of discipleship that St. John's tells itself reveals its self-understanding of spiritual formation.[2] As we will see later in the chapter, this self-understanding of spiritual formation is brought forward through social ties that bind people of faith together.

---

1. Hopewell, *Congregation*, para. 25.
2. Pseudonyms are used for the congregation and participants in this chapter.

Before the COVID-19 pandemic, St. John's average Sunday worship attendance was approximately two hundred people—a significant worship attendance for an Anglican parish in Canada.³ In an established neighborhood in a major city in Western Canada, St. John's is a parish with a long history that has an aging demographic but a good mix of young families. St. John's has a concern for the spiritual formation of its congregants and of its neighborhood. It is a welcoming community that has a concern for all types of diversities. This is the context of St. John's in which stories of spiritual formation and growth will be told. Before telling these stories, a word about theological method that provides a lens to better understand the stories.

Practical theology often begins with questions that stem from daily or common experiences. Osmer describes four core and interconnected tasks of practical theological interpretation that can be implemented to guide and respond to specific episodes, situations, or contexts in ministry for pastoral leaders:

> **Descriptive-empirical Task:** What is going on? Gathering information to better understand particular episodes, situations, or contexts.
>
> **Interpretive Task:** Why is this going on? Entering into a dialogue with the social sciences to interpret and explain why certain actions and patterns are taking place.
>
> **Normative Task:** What ought to be going on? Raising normative questions from the perspectives of theology, ethics, and/or practice.
>
> **Pragmatic Task:** How might we respond? Forming an action plan and undertaking specific responses that seek to shape the episode, situation, or context in desirable directions.⁴

In this chapter, I will use the interpretive and normative tasks as ways to narrate the stories of spiritual formation at St. John's. The interpretive task will use insights from sociology and psychology of religion to describe and explain the stories of spiritual formation at St. John's. The normative task addresses the cross-disciplinary dialogue between the social sciences and theology. Osmer identifies three models of cross-disciplinary dialogue as part of the normative task:

---

3. Anglican Church of Canada, "2017 Statistical Report," 1–9; Folkins, *Gone by 2040?*, 6–8.

4. Osmer, "Practical Theology," 2. For a concise description of Osmer's method see Osmer, *Practical Theology*.

1. Correlational Dialog: Theology and social sciences have mutual influence.

2. Transversal Dialog: An intersection and divergence of disciplines that share resources of rationality.

3. Transformational Dialog: Distinct language worlds requiring transformation, not simple translation.[5]

The stories of spiritual formation at St. John's seem to fall within the scope of Osmer's correlational model where the dialogue between theology and the social sciences "is one of mutual influence and critique, not a one-way monolog... where theology listens carefully to other disciplines and learns from them."[6] With this theological lens in mind, it is important to highlight two things: (1) how stories of spiritual formation are obtained at St. John's; and (2) a brief definition of spiritual formation/spiritual growth.

OBTAINING DISCIPLESHIP STORIES

With two research assistants (Kennedy Quantz and Phillip Blindenbach), nineteen congregants were interviewed, including eleven males and eight females ranging in age from thirty-five and ninety years old. The one-hour interviews were recorded and transcribed. The interview guide consisted of ten questions such as, In what ways would you say your parish is flourishing? And, What would you consider to be some challenges in your immediate horizon that could possibly limit your ability to flourish as a parish? Participant observations occurred with the parish council, small groups, Sunday worship services at 8:00 a.m. and 10:30 a.m., Christmas eve service, choral evensong, and Zoom coffee hours. Three focus groups with older adults occurred plus a morning Appreciative Inquiry event to identify key periods and experiences in parish history and the ways that the parish might move forward toward congregational flourishing. The highly organized parish archives provided excellent historical resources and data as well.

---

5. Osmer, *Practical Theology*, 172.
6. Osmer, *Practical Theology*, 172.

A BRIEF DEFINITION OF DISCIPLESHIP/SPIRITUAL FORMATION AND GROWTH

The theological and sociological literature define spiritual formation or spiritual growth in various ways. The term discipleship is contested and some theological sectors instead use terms such as "spiritual formation" or "faith formation."[7] With many definitions and terminologies, one common agreement in theological circles is that a disciple is a follower of Jesus who moves to some type of transformation or maturity in their Christian faith. Beyond this, the definition of discipleship diverges in a myriad of uses and meanings. This chapter will draw upon a sociological conception of spiritual growth as "a process that involves an expanding assessment and mastery of one's religious narrative and attachment to one's tradition, expressing itself through greater participation in corporate and private worship and institutional involvement."[8] As will become central later, the corporate aspects to spiritual growth at St. John's, notably the social ties and trust that members have with one another, are pivotal for people's spiritual formation. This flexible framework that deals with means and processes of cultivating spiritual growth is a useful entrance for making sense of a common perception and experience at St. John's regarding spiritual growth. As defined by one congregant,

> One of my favorite sayings about Anglicans, which I have heard on a couple of occasions, is we don't check our brain at the door. . . . It's okay to doubt and continue doubting and . . . wrestle with things and there's not a lot of dogma. And I always felt . . . the community that I entered was very much like that; there's a lot of searching and questing and uncertainty about the faith and what it all meant.

Put another way, this congregant's experience of spiritual growth captures the phenomenon as an evolving and fluid process.

---

7. Teo, "Christian Spiritual Formation," 138–140. Spiritual formation is defined differently depending on context. See ch. 6 for an example of a different story of spiritual formation.

8. Gallagher and Newton, "Defining Spiritual Growth," 237.

FOUR KEY STORYLINES OF SPIRITUAL FORMATION

From the nineteen interviews, one of the key storylines focused on various areas of spiritual formation and growth at both the individual and parish levels. One prominent storyline told by congregants was the importance of the liturgy, especially the music in the liturgy and Holy Communion, with "importance" meaning different things for congregants. For some, the liturgy was beautiful and mysterious that helps congregants turn their gaze toward God and connect to the soul. One congregant who serves in the choir put it this way:

> I remember at the very final chord of that anthem, so the chord just shot out over the over the congregation or over the audience, shall we say, and there's almost like an echo—something came back to me and the others, and what came back was, I think it might have been the listeners going wow, was sort of wow. And I find that frequently with a choir is that was the most sort of intense experience.... To me it was like a doorway into the great mystery. It's like that which is deeply powerful and deeply good but which we cannot explain!

Another congregant mentioned the importance of the Holy Communion for their spiritual growth:

> I also find strength in participating in the liturgy, most specifically in the communion ministry. I can't really explain my feelings in this regard, but what I do know is that the act of offering the bread and the wine, the host and the cup, is for me a very powerful act of love, executed in the context of believing in the force of good. It is an act of compassion that trumps all other kinds of connections that I might experience with my fellow human beings.

For others, the importance of the music in the liturgy provides a sense of identity for St. John's as a welcoming community. One older female congregant, on the importance of music, put it this way: "Well I think that first of all, there's some strong supports.... The music ministry at St. John's is important for many people and rightfully. I think that it is the people who are just welcoming—really welcoming!" Many of the people who initially attend St. John's and stay are hooked by the choral music in the worship service. The same congregant confessed, "And the music is just beautiful! So, the music really hooked me."

A second storyline from congregants is the importance of excellent preaching for spiritual growth. One interviewee says about one of its previous rector's abilities to exegete and apply the text,

> He was a master exegete! That guy could do things, like I'd sit there going . . . wow! That's pretty rare! People would know, like it was masterful! Man, he was just intuitive, did his research, and then turn[ed] that into something meaningful, right?

The homilies encouraged several congregants to think more clearly about the life of faith. One congregant put it this way: "I find [the rector's] style of the homily to be both thought provoking, and straightforward." As captured previously, another congregant said, "You know, one of my favorite sayings about Anglicans, which I have heard on a couple of occasions, is we don't check our brain at the door." These three quotations suggest that when it comes to spiritual growth, thoughtful preaching gives permission to doubt and that the setting at St. John's allows for spiritual searching and questing, which is part of the journey of faith.[9]

Third, congregants told stories of spiritual growth that happened in a Bible study or small group context. Before the COVID-19 pandemic, Bible study and small groups helped congregants better understand the faith. One congregant stated it this way: "It was nice to get together and talk to other people about . . . Christian beliefs[,] . . . going through the books and reading them, giving your opinion, hearing what other people thought of the same thing[,] . . . to have a group discussion that wasn't just sitting in church listening to a sermon." Learning with others in community seems to be important for many of the congregants. "The readings are short and contemplative. We will read a short chapter, contemplate it on our own for a week, meet and discuss it, then spend another week contemplating it before we start the next reading. It's not a great deal of reading but a ton of discussion."

It is this learning together through conversation and time to reflect on the learning that aids spiritual growth. Learning happens in these small groups and Bible studies because of the diverse people and personalities that make up the learning community and the respect and trust that develops. One congregant describes it this way:

> If you've been in groups like this[,] . . . there's three or four kinds of people in there. They're the ones that never say anything but

---

9. Shults and Sandage, *Transforming Spirituality*.

always attend and just listen. Then there's the ones that if you say something that they really disagree with, they'll speak up, and otherwise you don't hear them. And then there's the strong personalities, you know, they're always going to be saying something. And there's the others that'll participate sometimes. So, I would say, yeah, there was some strong personalities—very bright ones!

Congregants also spoke about trust in a small group context: "I think the trust comes from simply the shared, it's like, it's almost like, if I can't trust people here, who can I trust?" As mentioned above, spiritual formation includes the ability to ask questions and, at times, experience doubt. For St. John's, Bible study and small groups provide a context to ask questions, but the precondition for spiritual formation is trust and respect for one another.

From a theological perspective, trust and respect for one another that pay significant attention to relationality points to a practical theology of love that affirms that God is the origin of love. In other words, God's nature is love. Schieb nicely puts it this way:

> God's love creates a reciprocal bond; God's love makes our love of God and one another possible. . . . Love occurs in a relational context between subjects and intends the flourishing of the other. Any definition of love that shapes a pastoral theology of love must be grounded in this biblical witness to love as well as in human experiences of love.[10]

For congregants at St. John's, it seems that Bible study and small groups provided the relational context to express love for God and for others. It is through the Christian practice of Bible study and small groups that congregants respond "to God's grace by attending to human need in light of and through God's transformative love."[11]

The final storyline that congregants told concerned spiritual formation of young families, children, and youth, and generational diversity. Spiritual formation of children and youth were important ministries before the COVID-19 pandemic. During the pandemic, the parish lost the momentum of its ministries to young families, children, and youth. Many congregants pointed to the oral history project that showed St. John's had a vital history of working with children and families. The congregant interviews reinforced the importance of youth, family, and children's ministries—and the

10. Schieb, "Love," 710.
11. Schieb, "Love," 711.

strong connection with generational diversity—to the vitality of the parish. Congregants spoke of their personal experience of Sunday school and their own spiritual formation growing up. The older congregants described how when their children were young, they were involved in Sunday school, boys' and girls' choirs, and so forth.

Connected to family and children spiritual formation are aspirational stories of generational diversity. Many of the congregant interviews talked about having more generational diversity and ways to keep young families engaged with the parish. These conversations were often framed around discipleship and wishing for more young people to be involved at the parish. One parish council member put it this way:

> So [the rector and the rector's spouse] had a lot of energy around family and ministering and, being on the parish council, we would hear the sort of tally of, you know, so many new families! That was always very heartening to me because I sort of switched between a couple of different opinions on where the Anglican Church and St. John's Church in particular is going. I mean the demographics are not good.

As mentioned earlier, the congregant interviews indicate that generational diversity is connected to discipleship. Congregants often spoke about children's choir, Sunday school, and so forth, that develop children's spirituality.

At present, St. John's uses the Messy Church program as a way of being church in order for all ages to join in experiencing fun and faith formative activities. Based on the values of all ages together, celebration, creativity, hospitality, and Christ-centeredness, this program at St. John's aims to:

- To provide an opportunity for people of all ages to worship together
- To help people of all ages feel they belong in church and to each other
- To help people have fun and be creative together
- To introduce Jesus through hospitality, friendship, stories and worship[12]

In terms of the monthly Messy Church meetings, it typically includes a welcome; a creative time to explore the biblical theme with activities, games, and crafts; a celebration time involving storyline, prayer, and songs; and a

---

12. Messy Church Canada, "What Is Messy Church?," sec. 4.

STORIES OF SPIRITUAL FORMATION AND GROWTH

sit-down meal together at tables. The interview with the rector describes Messy Church in this way at St. John's:

> It was a Saturday evening, four o'clock to six o'clock or something like that, where we would gather down in the lower hall. And people would come in. We'd have a welcome and introduction to the theme for the evening. So, I can remember what the themes were that we use—something accessible for kids. And something we could build a whole bunch of crafts and activities around [and] setup around the hall for different stations. And after that welcoming orientation of a thing, families—whole families—from young kids . . . we are not much for teenagers . . . parents, grandparents, would just sort of go around to these different stations. So sometimes they're interactive games, sometimes they're crafts—all around the theme. So, it's all sort of feeding into whatever the theme for the evening is. And then once we've sort of done that for a while, we['d] gather all together again [and] we'd sing a song.

Despite St. John's attempt to reach out to families and children and youth, the rector and parish council leadership know they are competing with other organizations, such as sports teams and other family commitments, for people's time and resources. This competition of time was given as one of the reasons for some families and youth not regularly attending Sunday worship. This was affirmed by the observational comments of older interviewees and by many of the congregants who have young families. St. John's is not alone in these perceptions. Steve McMullin's 2013 research reveals that pastors and members in congregations declining in size typically attribute their reduced worship attendance to competing demands among congregants.[13] As a whole, St. John's is concerned for the spiritual formation of their children, families, and youth because of an aging demographic. To put it bluntly, they want to see a next generation. This former parish council member highlights it this way: "The last year that I was on parish council, we had more baptisms than funerals! And that was a really big deal to us. We were baptizing more than we were burying."

As you hear these refrains regarding music, preaching, Bible studies and small groups, and children and youth, which of these areas would you say are strengths in your own congregation in spurring spiritual formation and growth among your parishioners and why? Are there certain demographics you would say resonate more with some of these formative

13. McMullin, "Secularization of Sunday."

dynamics in your church? Are there demographics you'd like to see more of in your church who potentially are less inclined to connect with your congregation's music or preaching, for example? If you were to adapt how you approached some of these ministry areas, what risks would you need to take, relationally, theologically, or practically, and would those risks be worth it in your mind? My hope is that by seriously entertaining questions such as these, you and those in your congregation might envision possible paths forward to strengthen your church's capacity to richly and meaningfully disciple and spiritually form those who call your church their "home" faith community.

SPIRITUAL FORMATION AND RELIGIOUS SOCIAL NETWORKS

What ties these four storylines together to make for a cohesive narrative at St. John's? Relationality and connection are the "glue." To use another image, relationality is like a tapestry, as one of the congregants mentioned: "I would say the interpersonal connections are both the warp and weft of keeping it all together as a tapestry. I think those interpersonal connections are absolutely critical." At St. John's, discipleship happens in an atmosphere of community and relationship building. Discipleship happens in relationships and knowing the other. One couple talked about this social nature of discipleship:

> So, I just really bonded with the community pretty quickly and over the years. I served on parish council. I'm a lector, a greeter. [My spouse], pre COVID, [my spouse] was a Sunday school teacher. We're in charge of the stampede breakfast. And because we both have a hospitality background, if there are big social events, we're normally either involved or at least consulted. We really like to get involved in the social stuff.

In building community, it helps to develop religious social networks that aid in spiritual growth. By religious social networks, I mean social ties that bind people of faith together.[14] Congregants who have strong ties are reluctant to lose them compared with those who have sparse ties because, as Rodney Stark points out, "people with strong ties are happier and even healthier, because in such networks members provide one another with

---

14. Everton, "Networks and Religion."

strong emotional and material support in times of grief or trouble and someone with whom to share life's joys and triumphs."[15]

What do religious social networks do and how do they help in spiritual growth? Empirical research on religious social networks suggests that belonging to a group such as a congregation is an important and powerful need.[16] In fact, a congregant's affective ties to a congregation in the form of friendship can be a determining reason for adhering to theological beliefs[17] and heightening religiosity in participating in religious activities (i.e., volunteerism).[18] An older female congregant spoke about building friendships with younger people:

> I think it's important to develop relationships with younger people. I've always found people younger than I to be interesting. I've made a real effort to single people out in the congregation and develop personal relationships with them. Often those lead to conversations about important life stuff but also spiritual insights. I mentioned walking with a guy who's almost twenty years younger than I am just a couple of days ago, and we were able to talk about some difficult stuff because we built this relationship based on a common understanding of spiritual values—not in any complicated ultra-religious way but spiritual values.

This lengthy quote is an example of how strong social ties begin and develop in a congregational context around common spiritual values. As previously mentioned, this may lead to a heightened sense of religiosity in the form of discipleship. For example, congregant A describes his regular interactions with congregant B (as they both served together in the parish choir) and of the way in which congregant B eventually would ask congregant A to serve in a weekly discipleship program that happened prior to the worship service:

> And if you think of it, every Thursday and every Sunday, plus all the holidays, I would see [congregant B]. He was somebody I would see at least twice a week. . . . At break time, we have a cup of tea, or we used to have all these communal things, a cup of tea [and a] lemon square [to talk]. So, he must have got an idea in

---

15. Stark, *Sociology*, 37.

16. Ammerman, *Congregations*, 562–81; Lim and Putnam, "Religion"; Maslow, *Motivation and Personality*; Putnam, *Bowling Alone*; Stroope, "Culture Shapes Community."

17. Stroope, "Social Networks."

18. Merino, "Religious Social Networks."

his mind that I might be good at preparing the upcoming week [for the discipleship program,] which typically was the café style where we would invite a guest speaker before the 10:30 service and afterwards we would be discussing who the next speaker would be and what they would bring to the congregation spiritually.

At St. John's, religious social networking in the form of relationality or friendship creates a sense of belonging. This sense of belonging that comes from strong social ties in the form of friendship connects with a congregant's emotional sense of feeling "safe" so that spiritual maturity can occur.[19]

In the next chapter we'll read of one congregation's powerful experiences that nurture spiritual formation *and* social ties. Before getting there, however, as you think about the link between social ties and spiritual formation in your church context, would you say this is an area of strength or an opportunity for growth? What aspects of your congregation's story—past, present, and future—alongside the culture, leader-follower dynamics, interpersonal experiences, and overall structure of your church, help or hinder members' abilities to foster meaningful social ties with one another? Returning once more to the Flourishing Congregations Construct, factors such as hospitable community, leaders who empower and equip others to lead, and engaged laity, where there is a shared ownership of congregational life, can all go a long way to draw members into deeper community with one another.[20] My encouragement is to think holistically about the interconnectedness of these congregational realities that, together, can amplify your church's ability to flourish in the area of spiritual formation.

SOCIAL TIES AND THE FOUR STORYLINES

Strong social ties bring the four storylines together. The importance of liturgy (e.g., music, Holy Communion), preaching, and Bible study/small group provide not only important pathways for spiritual growth but also opportunities for regular social interaction that builds community. One congregant puts it this way, "I think humans like and need community. I think that the parish builds . . . through music and worship, through a sense of camaraderie and connection with people in the church, and through the ability to attract and retain good clergy over the years." Collective participation in these spiritual growth pathways seem to build interpersonal

---

19. McAlpine et al., *Signs of Life*.
20. McAlpine et al., *Signs of Life*.

feelings of mutuality and trust. In other words, the more congregants interact with one another, the more likely they are to develop emotional ties of closeness.[21]

With respect to the fourth storyline and spiritual formation of children and youth, the parish archives and the Appreciative Inquiry event tell stories that whenever St. John's provides significant pastoral and lay leadership to children and youth ministries, there was a critical mass of youth and children in the parish. These two factors—pastoral and lay leadership and a cohort of youth and children—happen in cycles at St. John's. One older congregant put it this way as he reflected back to a flourishing period of when there was a cohort of children who attended youth and children ministries: "Well, the [kids in] youth group [were] kids of baby boomers. I think it was just a cohort. I think there was just a natural cohort of ten to twenty families, and they are now in their early 70s. I'm in my early 60s. So, when our kids were coming up, there was sort of a natural feed to the youth group and so our kids benefited from this cohort and the kids were semi-interested or interested in attending."

As was captured in the Flourishing Congregations Construct, and then again in the stories at St. Jerome's (chapter 2) and St. Eustace's (chapter 3), leadership matters to congregational flourishing. At St. John's, when there is a significant presence of pastoral and lay leadership in these ministry areas, structure and programs for children and youth tend to follow. With good cohort numbers of children and youth, these programs and structures provided opportunities for children and youth at St. John's to not only address spiritual formation issues but also to build strong social ties in the form of friendships that keep youth and children attending these ministries. The opposite seems true from a parent who made this sobering observation of her children:

> They were unfortunate in their cohort of the church.... There were almost no other kids in their age and in kindergarten, especially for [one of my children]. So, there's a whole whack load of kids that came in, you know, just a bit younger than [this child]. That's unfortunate, they never really made friendships, which, so that's why I'm like, okay, let's bring your friends to the church. You know, it's my way of trying to make up for that. But that was unfortunate, because [children] think that makes a big difference that they can make strong friendships. And that hasn't happened.

21. Ellison and George, "Religious Involvement."

At present, St. John's seems to be in a cycle where there is a pastor for children, youth, and family ministries, with many children and some youth attending the parish.

CONCLUSION

In this chapter, four narratives emerge of the important processes and mechanisms that facilitated spiritual growth at St. John's. Worship, preaching, and Bible study/small groups are all important means and practices for spiritual growth, but just as important, and that which is not emphasized as much in the theological literature and pastoral practice, is the parish environment and context in which spiritual formation happens. Community is important but when that is unpacked further, we see the importance of social ties in the form of friendships. In the fourth narrative with children, youth, and families, a community where friendship can be made not only keeps youth and children interested and connected to St. John's, but it also strengthens the likelihood for spiritual growth to occur.

QUESTIONS FOR REFLECTION

1. What are the stories of spiritual formation in your congregation?
2. How would you describe the culture of spiritual formation in your congregation? Is it alive and well, dormant, non-existent, or somewhere in-between?
3. How well does your congregation address the life tasks, needs, interests, and spiritual-religious life of children, adolescents, young adults, midlife adults, mature adults, and older adults? Where are the areas of strength? Where are the areas for growth?
4. Where are the strong social ties built and maintained in your congregation that bring congregants together to create community?
5. What are the strengths, plus areas for development, in intergenerational relationships, community, and spiritual formation?

BIBLIOGRAPHY

Ammerman, Nancy. "Congregations: Local, Social, and Religious." In *The Oxford Handbook of the Sociology of Religion*, edited by Peter B. Clarke, 562–81. New York: Oxford University Press, 2009.

Anglican Church of Canada. "2017 Statistical Report." Anglican Church of Canada, last updated Dec. 18, 2019. https://www.anglican.ca/wp-content/uploads/2017-ACC-Stats.pdf.

Ellison, Christopher, and Linda George. "Religious Involvement, Social Ties, and Social Support in a Southeastern Community." *Journal for the Scientific Study of Religion* 33 (1994) 46–61.

Everton, Sean. "Networks and Religion: Ties that Bind, Loose, Build Up, and Tear Down." *Journal of Social Structure* 16 (2015) 1–34.

Folkins, Tali. "Gone by 2040?" *Anglican Journal* 146 (2020) 6–8.

Gallagher, Sally, and Chelsea Newton. "Defining Spiritual Growth: Congregations, Community, and Connectedness." *Sociology of Religion* 70 (2009) 232–61. https://academic.oup.com/socrel/article-abstract/70/3/232/1655207.

Hopewell, James. *Congregations: Stories and Structures*. Philadelphia: Fortress, 1984. https://www.religion-online.org/book/congregation-stories-and-structures/.

Lim, Chaeyopon, and Robert Putnam. "Religion, Social Networks, and Life Satisfaction." *American Sociological Review* 75 (2010) 914–33.

Maslow, Abraham. *Motivation and Personality*. New York: Harper, 1954.

McAlpine, Bill, et al. *Signs of Life: Catholic, Mainline, and Conservative Protestant Congregations in Canada*. Toronto: Tyndale Academic, 2021.

McMullin, Steve. "The Secularization of Sunday: Real or Perceived Competition for Churches." *Review of Religious Research* 55 (2013) 43–59.

Merino, Stephen. "Religious Social Networks and Volunteering: Examining Recruitment via Close Ties." *Review of Religious Research* 55 (2013) 509–27.

Messy Church Canada. "What Is Messy Church?" https://messychurch.ca/about/.

Osmer, Richard. "Practical Theology: A Current International Perspective." *HTS Theological Studies* 67 (2011) 1–7.

———. *Practical Theology: An Introduction*. Grand Rapids: Eerdmans, 2008.

Putnam, Robert. *Bowling Alone: The Collapse and Revival of American Community*. New York: Simon and Schuster, 2000.

Scheib, Karen. "Love as a Starting Point for Pastoral Theological Reflection." *Pastoral Psychology* 63 (2014) 705–17.

Shults, F. Le Ron, and Steven Sandage. *Transforming Spirituality: Integrating Theology and Psychology*. Grand Rapids: Baker Academic, 2006.

Stark, Rodney. *Sociology*. 10th ed. Belmont, CA: Wadsworth, 2007.

Stroope, Samuel. "How Culture Shapes Community: Bible Belief, Theological Unity, and a Sense of Belonging in Religious Congregations." *Sociological Quarterly* 52 (2011) 568–92.

———. "Social Networks and Religion: The Role of Congregational Social Embeddedness in Religious Belief and Practice." *Sociology of Religion* 73 (2012) 273–98.

Teo, Wilson. "Christian Spiritual Formation." *Emerging Leadership Journeys* 10 (2017) 138–50.

6

Resonant Relationships
Spiritual Formation as a Congregational Focus

Mark Chapman, Andrea Chang, and James Watson

INTRODUCTION

STILL WATERS IS A small, Chinese, evangelical congregation in the Toronto area that has a story of what it describes as loving "the LORD Jesus with all her mind, heart, and spirit in wholeness."[1] This vision effectively shapes what Still Waters does and how it does it. This chapter explores how this founding vision, and its resultant supportive spiritual formation emphasis, shaped the development of the church and the lives of its participants into a story of *resonant relationships* with God and with others. Resonant relationship is a term that can be used to describe an uncontrollable, responsive relationship that leads to transformation. We start by telling the story of Still Waters, then we use a theory about how humans relate to the world (identified here as resonance) to help us understand why Still Waters is flourishing.

---

1. The name of the church and the names of research participants have been replaced with pseudonyms for their privacy. Quotations are from the church website unless otherwise specified.

FOUNDING VISION AND RESONANT RELATIONSHIPS

The story of how Still Waters is flourishing through resonant relationships starts with their vision

> that the body of Christ was to live under the lordship and heart of the Good Shepherd, Jesus Christ. This new church of God was aimed to follow, model after, and preach Christ Jesus until His return. The chosen name, [Still Waters], reflected very much their Spirit-led core values. The vision of the [church] directed her pilgrimage journey towards a specific Christian spirituality: that the church should love the LORD Jesus with all her mind, heart, and spirit in wholeness.

Consistent with the "self-identity" aspect of the Flourishing Congregations Construct, this vision points to some of the emphases that are core to the church's story. It identifies their understanding of themselves as focused on a contemplative approach to spirituality that accentuates resonant relationships with God and others. While this includes well-known church practices such as communal prayer, Bible study, and preaching, it also emphasizes practices such as solitude, silence, and contemplative Bible reading (*lectio divina*). Nurturing the spiritual life ("love the LORD Jesus with all her mind, heart, and spirit in wholeness") flows through everything they do. It is featured on their website, all the documents we reviewed reference it, and everyone we spoke to (pastors and congregants) highlighted it as the core of who they are as the people of God. Their emphasis on being moved by ("under" Christ) and responding to God ("pilgrimage journey") toward transformation ("spiritual wholeness") are characteristics of resonant relationships.

THE STORY OF STILL WATERS

Still Waters is an evangelical Protestant, multilingual, multigenerational, Chinese church. There are a range of ages, structures, and processes to minister to different demographic groups; a straightforward Sunday service; attentiveness to the three different languages spoken by congregants; and attention paid to discipleship and the local community. The fifty-five to sixty people attending on a Sunday morning might be speaking Mandarin, English, or Cantonese, or move between these different languages as needed, all in the same service. All ministry at Still Waters takes place in all three languages. In some cases, our researchers relied on local participants for translation and to explain what was taking place. Just over half the attendees on Sunday are over fifty-five, but the pattern changes at monthly events where just over half are children under twelve. Some of their events are youth and community oriented (e.g., youth tutoring). Most church events take place in the building they have owned since 2008.

The genesis of Still Waters' emphasis on spiritual formation is rooted in an observation made by the pastoral couple that, after five years of preaching the word and teaching the Bible, they personally were missing something. After they sought out spiritual direction for themselves, they realized that if they, as leaders, were missing a deeper experience in their spirituality then their congregants would be too. So they adjusted their approach to ministry to include more focus on spiritual disciplines. When they collaborated with several close connections to start a new church, they gravitated toward spiritual formation. In 2000 they started to meet in a Salvation Army building and launched Still Waters with an emphasis on spiritual disciplines.

Spiritual disciplines, explains Adele Ahlberg Calhoun, "are intentional ways we open space in our lives for the worship of God."[2] A spiritual discipline is a way of being present with God. These disciplines can also be understood as spiritual practices and include the specific actions one takes to live out that discipline.[3] Spiritual disciplines and related practices are means to help us encounter God and become more like Jesus. Still Waters puts particular emphasis on disciplines such as silence and solitude. They also include more common ministries such as Bible study, "pulpit teaching," lay training, and more, but both spiritual-formation-oriented ministries and more common ministries aim to "shape passion for loving God and neighbor."

In 2005 they leaned even further into spiritual formation by blending spiritual direction, pastoral counseling, and biblical teaching (which they call "cognitive Word formation") into all church teaching, including preaching and training seminars (see below for more details). Their website depicts this as a factor in their subsequent thriving. Specifically they explain that "heading towards the vision of a refined holistic Christian spirituality, the [church] started to grow in number, finance, and fruits of life in Christ." In 2009 they bought their own building which they describe as a turning point in their ability to organize their church around spiritual formation

2. Calhoun, *Spiritual Disciplines*, 22.
3. Calhoun, *Spiritual Disciplines*.

because it provided consistent space for church activities such as prayer meetings and Taizé services (an approach to contemplative worship that started in Taizé France).[4]

From 2010 to the present there has been "ongoing effort in the renewal of holistic spiritual formation." This can be seen in the use of their building for silent retreats and training and in a growing children's ministry. In 2022 they hired an assistant pastor who immediately pursued studies to become a spiritual director. They are renovating their building to further serve the needs of spiritual formation. This renovation, with an architectural design that reflects their founding vision, sets the stage for resonant relationship. The renovated building will have lots of small rooms for prayer and silence and other contemplative spiritual disciplines. It will facilitate holding retreat-like events in the building. Several participants were clear that the building was the means not the destination of their efforts. They are renovating their building to better serve their vision of "wholistic Christian spirituality." They do not see the building as being able to control or instigate spiritual experience, rather, it will contribute to an environment where resonant relationships with God can be fostered.

This building renovation is in line with Still Water's written history, which serves as a key foundational document for how they understand themselves. It emphasizes "wholistic Christian spirituality" with particular attention to "disciplines of abstinence." Disciplines of abstinence help people make space to listen to God by temporarily removing something from one's life. For example, disciplines such as "solitude, silence, centering prayers, group retreats, group *Lectio Divina*," Taizé services, Bible contemplation, spiritual direction, and other practices that involve abstaining from regular activity to intentionally invest in time listening to God. Other examples of activities contributing to wholeness are services focused on contemplation, the provision of spiritual direction, and a lot of emphasis on quietness, singing, and silence at the annual retreat. At the retreat everyone is divided into groups with a leader who is responsible to make sure everyone in their group is involved and cared for. They are very aware of how the different ages, the different languages spoken, and the experiences of being brought up in different locations have given their community different perspectives on life and on church. They work hard to make sure that all these diverse voices are included by assuring that people can participate in multiple languages. The emphasis is on transformation through relationship.

---

4. For more on Taizé, see "Taizé."

The senior and lead pastors, a married couple who have different roles at the church, are both trained in spiritual formation in both Roman Catholic and evangelical seminaries and have made spiritual formation the core of their ministries. They are both spiritual directors and provide this service for congregants. In this context, spiritual direction is the spiritual accompaniment of someone toward a posture of listening to God and orienting one's life toward God's purposes. The church has an expectation that every adult participates in spiritual direction. Receiving spiritual direction is not required to be part of the congregation but is required before congregants can get further training. It is offered at their annual spiritual retreats, and other primarily contemplative spiritual disciplines are encouraged through spiritual direction. One of their pastors explained that "spiritual formation is not the change of habits but it's the change of heart" and later described it as aligning the inner person to "the inner life of the LORD Jesus." He further explained that "the main teaching part of this church is not from the sermon. It is from spiritual formation training."

They recognize that, to practice spiritual disciplines, individuals must be introduced to them and taught how to use them. This manifests most obviously in contemplative practices such as *lectio divina*, spiritual direction, and the robust program of formation-oriented training supporting such practices. This training includes attention to biblical knowledge and its application in church actions (e.g., worship services, retreats, community care). To foster these disciplines, as people get more involved in the church they are encouraged to take church-run training that aims toward spiritual wholeness. Reflective of structures and processes that are integral to congregational flourishing, the pastors lead formal training in areas of spiritual formation that are sequentially organized according to participation in congregational life. They offer courses that lead to baptism (as a milestone in personal commitment to faith and the church), followed by post-baptismal development of spiritual disciplines, a course to prepare congregants for service, and then training in biblical interpretation as preparation for leadership. All these courses have a Bible study element but also put a large amount of emphasis on spiritual disciplines and their sustained practice—that is, it is not sufficient to learn about the spiritual disciplines; the courses also involve the practice of spiritual disciplines. For example, one of the requirements to become a leader in the church includes going on a silent retreat, which is not common in other evangelical churches. Spiritual disciplines are not a way to control God but a way to enter resonant relationship with God. One pastor explained, "There is no instant noodles when it comes to spiritual direction ministry. It's not a counseling session that fixes the problem at the end of this session. Spiritual direction is a totally different ministry. You don't even see the fruit sometimes." Participants understood this training as a strong commitment of the congregation to collective spiritual growth over the long term.

This description of Still Waters shows a church that is flourishing in many of the ways identified by the Flourishing Congregations Construct. In its organizational ethos it has a clear self-identity and it has visionary leadership with a clear focus and will to guide the congregation. It is innovative with the intentional integration of elements of spiritual disciplines into communal activities. They have developed clear structures and processes for these activities. Internally it emphasizes discipleship and hospitality in its welcoming of community children, and it has an engaged and somewhat diverse laity. Externally it has little emphasis on classic approaches to evangelism but does care about the salvation of the people it engages, and it attends to neighborhood involvement. However, there is something going on across these different characteristics of flourishing churches that is less about what they are doing than how they are doing it. The concept of resonance helps describe this dynamic, which we turn to next. As we do so, think about what role spiritual formation currently plays in the life of your church and what role could it take in the future? In what ways would you say you are flourishing or floundering in this regard? How might you adjust structures and processes to make spiritual formation an ethos rather than a program?

RESONANCE

As we spent more time with Still Waters, we began to think about how this approach to church seems well suited to address several contemporary cultural challenges. The concept of resonance developed by sociologist Harmut Rosa offers a good way to explore the significance of their story. Resonance, according to Rosa, is a responsive relationship to the world in which we live that leads to transformation.[5] It is a way of being in the world.[6] This orientation around resonance (being) rather than resources or programs (doing) at Still Waters is rooted in its vision of a church with

---

5. Rosa, *Resonance*, 298.
6. Rosa, *Resonanz*, 285, referenced in Susen, "Resonance of Resonance," 313.

a focus on the spiritual formation of the whole community. It draws from a contemplative approach to spiritual formation and makes extensive use of classic spiritual disciplines as means to the formation of congregants. In Rosa's terminology it emphasizes both horizontal relationships, which are meaningful interactions between people—akin to social ties discussed at St. John's in the previous chapter—and vertical relationships, which are more "'transcendent' spheres of engagement."[7]

Given this, what is the context in which Still Waters and other contemporary churches operate? James K. A. Smith explains that, for most of us, our lives are framed "entirely within a natural (rather than a supernatural) order."[8] Our default way of understanding reality is natural instead of supernatural. This is not to say that God talk is absent or that God is not relevant to people's lives, but God is sometimes rationalized and confined to personally controlled devotion (rather than devotion that is responsive to God's direction). The work of the church happens within the constraints of secular culture.[9] Churches seek to accumulate resources (e.g., money, buildings, people) as a sign of success, people become instruments for the goal of growth, and innovation is treated as an inherent good.[10] We try to control all possibilities so we can manufacture the outcome we are looking for. We fool ourselves into believing we have that degree of control. Andrew Root argues that ultimately such an approach to being church leads to exhaustion and alienation, what he calls the "fatigue d'être eglise."[11] We are tired of being the church.

Andrew Root explains that the antidote to this problem is resonance. He describes resonance as "a journey of seeking a narrative of connection to the world and those in the world who call out to us."[12] Resonance, explains Rosa, "is a mode of relating to the world in which the subject feels touched, moved, or addressed by the people, place, objects, etc. he or she encounters."[13] Resonance is the sense of connection that makes one "feel alive," which then leads to feeling *"called out to act."*[14] We feel moved,

---

7. Rosa, *Resonanz*, 419, referenced in Susen, "Resonance of Resonance," 316.
8. Smith, *How (Not) to Be Secular*, 141.
9. Root, *Congregation*; see also Taylor, *Secular Age*.
10. Root, *Church after Innovation*.
11. Root, *Congregation*, 13–16.
12. Root, *Congregation*, 216.
13. Rosa, "Available," 47, quoted in Root, *Congregation*, 196.
14. Root, *Congregation*, 200, 205 (emphasis original).

we respond, we are transformed, but the experience is elusive and uncontrollable.[15] This is a story about how humans encounter the world, and how the posture of the church as an institution can serve the God/human relationship. While a church exists in the natural world, the collective and individual experience of reflection and relationship with one another and with a God that cannot be explained brings resonance that can sustain and transform a congregation.

These are resonant relationships because they can lead us to feel touched or moved by another in such a way that we respond and are transformed. But, as these are relationships, we do not control others. We need to maintain an ongoing mutually caring relationship with each other. Spiritual formation seeks just such a relationship with God. We cannot control God, but spiritual disciplines provide the setting and the means to develop a resonant relationship. The story of Still Waters, from founding to contemporary practice, sets the stage for resonant relationships.

RESONANT RELATIONSHIPS WITH GOD AND WITH OTHERS

A resonant relationship is a relationship that helps us relate to the world in a way that helps us experience God and thus makes us feel alive as we encounter the God who is beyond us (a God who is transcendent). A church that values resonant relationships does not treat people instrumentally as resources that help the church grow, do ministry, and so forth. Growth or ministry are not pursued for their own sake or to control outcomes but are encountered as the natural outflow of resonant relationships. Individuals seek both a resonant relationship with God and resonant relationships with one another. However, in regular conversation at Still Waters participants often intertwined them together. This can be seen in the description of their vision and approach to spiritual formation.

Resonance is a responsive relationship with others and with God that moves us to response such that we are transformed. That such relationships are uncontrollable is what makes them valuable to us. Their very elusiveness drives us to continue to work on the relationships because when we are experiencing the mutuality of such relationships and are changed, we feel fully alive. Having explored resonance more generally this section looks at it in the context of Still Waters, using Rosa's four characteristics of resonance: moved, response, transformed, and uncontrollable. As you read these, give thought

15. Bjørn, "Acceleration and Resonance," 3.

to what the concept of resonant relationships might mean for your congregation, including the spoken and unspoken theological, relational, and practical assumptions you and those around you bring to your church's ministry. How might these assumptions change, in light of following characteristics?

Moved

To be moved is to be affected by another. "Something calls to us, moves us from without, and becomes important to us for its own sake."[16] Root says we have a sense of "feeling alive."[17]

Such relationships don't just happen. Rather they are fostered through the kind of activities encouraged by Still Waters: shared experiences, including mentorship like relationships such as spiritual direction, group experiences like retreats, a training structure that fosters these relationships, and individual attentiveness to God. When asked about what has led to the strong commitment individuals have to the church, one participant started by talking about the teaching ministry but then pivoted immediately to fostering a relationship with God. This pattern of storytelling was common among our participants and points to how they are moved by God and by other people.

Response

Being moved leads to a response. We reach out to that which moves us. We feel connected to the world because we can affect it.[18] Root calls this being "*called out to act.*"[19] One of the pastors explains, "I notice that, when the church focuses on prayer and relationship with God and also being in the word of God, people are self-perpetuating [in their spiritual health]." He goes on to explain that people need the church and one another to get to this stage of a self-perpetuating relationship with God. It is a sort of mutually reinforcing relationship between God and the community. Something this pastor calls "we and God." Another church member explains, "I hope that everyone including myself keeps that relationship with God and that

---

16. Rosa, *Uncontrollability*, 32. Rosa, *Uncontrollability*, 32.
17. Root, *Congregation*, 199.
18. Rosa, *Uncontrollability*, 32.
19. Root, *Congregation*, 205 (emphasis original).

sense of grace all the time—[to] be willing to every day cleanse their heart before the LORD because without that we're running around and doing a lot of things. That way we can grow as a church inside out."

Looking to the future, they are excited about the possibilities the renovated building offers. They remain as committed as ever to the original spiritual formation emphasis of the church and are returning to prepandemic activities that were much loved, such as communal meals and spiritual retreats. Here again we see an emphasis on resonant relationships as one of the defining features of the congregation—congregants are moved to response. Situating this concept in your context, how can you foster an atmosphere where your congregants are moved to response?

Transformed

Being moved and then responding transforms us. We are changed by our encounter with others. It is this change that brings the sense of feeling alive.[20] As we are affected by others, we respond in a way that leads to our transformation.[21]

It is in this sense that spiritual disciplines at Still Waters are not an end in themselves. The communal nature of how they practice spiritual disciplines provides avenues for being affected and transformed by each other. The church recognizes that spiritual disciplines aim to develop self-perpetuating relationships with God. Spiritual disciplines contribute to spiritual health. The church's perception is that those who actively engage in spiritual direction are more spiritually healthy than those who do not. One congregant testified that regular spiritual direction helps her repent, refocus, and serve. Spiritual disciplines help to counter our culture of individualism. For example, explains another participant, healthy forms of self-denial and discipline help to keep one's job or lifestyle from becoming an idol. Spiritual disciplines provide the resources and the motivation for active involvement (service) inside and outside the church. This is true even when they experience the benefit (e.g., transformation) but don't articulate the specific practice that led to that benefit (e.g., fasting). Spiritual disciplines enable a move toward God and a responsive relationship with God that contributes to transformation.

---

20. Rosa, *Uncontrollability*, 34.
21. Rosa, *Uncontrollability*, 35.

Transformation manifests in action. This is clear in participant's regular reference to a variety of spiritual disciplines drawn largely from contemplative spirituality (e.g., spiritual direction, silence, biblical contemplation, meditation, fasting, prayer, group spiritual retreats, community discernment). Such practices seem to encourage the active engagement of laity in the church. Lay people participate in everything from teaching to building maintenance. Participants often mentioned commitment not just to the church but to the vision of spiritual growth in the community. This message is reinforced by training that emphasizes the church vision and their organizational culture, which is focused on spiritual formation. Everyone is expected to do something. This vision extends to hospitality both inside and outside the church. They actively get together for meals, visit seniors, bring gifts to the isolated, and care for children through informal connections and formal programs like tutoring and scheduled individual contact. These findings remind us of the interconnectedness between the various dimensions of the Flourishing Congregations Construct, where what happens in one aspect of congregational life (e.g., discipleship) has a ripple effect in other areas (e.g., engaged laity, hospitable community, or neighborhood involvement). Of course, a central assumption within this construct is that intentionality—that is, structures and process—are integral for the things a congregation believes are most important. As such, how might the structures and processes of your church be supporting or restricting transformation?

Uncontrollability

We can set the conditions in which being moved to response and thus transformed is possible, but the outcome is ultimately uncontrollable. The experience is elusive, even if real when we encounter it. Resonance "cannot be manufactured or engineered."[22] Even when we try to "listen and respond" we may remain "unaffected and unable to make a connection."[23] Yet, even as it cannot be forced it also cannot be prevented and can show up in unexpected ways.[24]

For example, Still Waters does not understand itself as an outward looking church. They do not draw participants from the immediate

22. Rosa, *Uncontrollability*, 36.
23. Rosa, *Uncontrollability*, 36.
24. Rosa, *Uncontrollability*, 37.

neighborhood around the church, which is increasingly Middle Eastern, and no one mentioned partnerships with any other organizations. Furthermore, several participants expressed concern about their competencies in outreach and evangelism. However, an examination of their actual actions suggests that this might be an artifact of how they talk about themselves because they do engage in many activities that could be considered outward focused (e.g., seniors and children's ministries), which lead to uncontrollable results from being moved to response (e.g., greater connection with families because of pandemic tutoring). Still Water's emphasis on resonant relationships leads naturally to active care for others inside and outside the church. Resonance implies cooperation and collaboration because the other cannot be controlled. As you read these paragraphs, in what way(s) does the idea that we cannot control outcomes possibly free you and your ministry?

CONCLUSION: HOW RESONANCE IS A HELPFUL CONCEPT

Resonance is helpful for thinking about ministry because it gives us language to talk about what is going on in the life of the church without just talking about what we do. It gives us language to articulate the relational and uncontrollable nature of ministry. The life of the church is relational. This is captured in the oft-mentioned paraphrase of the great commandment as love God and love others. In relationship we are moved by others and in turn respond to them. It is in this interplay that people are transformed. Likewise, we recognize that as we are moved by and respond to God, we are transformed. It is in that process that we enter a fulfilled life, a life where we can feel fully alive and like we are where we are supposed to be. But this experience is elusive. We can set the stage for relationship, but we do not control others and we do not control God. It is this very uncontrollability that makes relationship worthwhile.

Still Waters sets the stage for resonance rather than controllability. They are not trying to control others and God. The life of the church organized around spiritual formation brings people within reach of God and one another as they seek to ground themselves in God through spiritual disciplines, teaching, and communal activity. They are setting the stage for the possibility of resonance. To develop a thriving community like that which Still Waters has developed is not to duplicate their structures and programs. Rather one pursues a vision of loving God and loving others.

Still Waters looks to the history of the church for a vision of a church oriented around spiritual formation. Rather than a church organized around resources and programs (to control the world), Still Waters is organized around spiritual formation—which they understand as being a change of the "heart with their LORD Jesus" (an uncontrollable relationship). The founding vision laid out a story of a church organized around a resonant relationship with God. Contemporary practice and congregation self-identity demonstrate that this vision remains the core identity of the church. To support this vision, they engage in spiritual disciplines that fit a posture of contemplative spirituality. They embrace practical forms of spiritual formation and respond to contemporary culture. They are led by a married couple who lead them to strongly value resonant relationships with God and between people more than resource accumulation. Together they try to draw on the skills and gifting of the whole community, try to get everybody in the congregation to participate in the activities of the church and contribute to the actions of the church, pay a lot of attention to children, care deeply about the spiritual transformation of their congregants, and, finally, are guided by their specific vision, which they let set boundaries on what they do and don't do. Their organizational ethos derives directly from this vision of themselves. As they narrate their self-identity, they describe how this vision of Still Waters is the story of the church. Each individual participant identified with the contemplative practices encouraged by the church (e.g., spiritual direction, silence) as much as with the collective activities of the church (e.g., services, Bible study). Resonant relationships with God and others take priority. All of this would not have been sustained over the twenty-two years of the life of the church without strong established structures and processes to help it grow and thrive in a particular direction. Their structures and processes do not control the outcomes but set the context in which the desired outcomes of spiritual formation can be fostered.

Still Waters has a structure and process to maintain and develop their ministry. Such systems are maintained by communicating their vision to new people who arrive, helping existing congregants articulate that vision, and applying it to decide on appropriate activities for the church. A strong vision of what the church is to be, combined with clearly practiced processes to maintain that vision, contributes to resonant relationships with God and with others. A well understood structure to hold this vision leads to active engagement with those around them.

Such resonant relationships are relationships that move us to respond to others such that we are changed. We do not control and cannot manufacture this result, but we can set the stage for such relationships to be possible. These experiences of God and each other make us feel alive because of an encounter with something beyond ourselves. It is the very uncontrollability of God and others that makes relationships have impact, because the give and take of the encounter is freely given. It is this experience that motivates individuals and churches to act according to God's purposes. Together these are prime factors in the flourishing of this congregation and a potent approach for other congregations to explore.

QUESTIONS FOR REFLECTION

1. How does your church prioritize some approaches to church over others?
2. What is the value of having an orienting vision that guides what your church does and does not do?
3. If your church has an orienting vision, how do the actions of your church match the vision to which God has called it?
4. How might the concept of resonance help you identify areas to develop in the spiritual formation of your congregation?
5. Are attempts to control outcomes getting in the way of relationships with God and with others in your ministry? If so, what changes might you make to move toward resonant relationships?

BIBLIOGRAPHY

Bjørn, Schermer. "Acceleration and Resonance: An Interview with Hartmut Rosa." *Acta Sociologica* 25.3 (2017) 1–7. https://journals.sagepub.com/pb-assets/cmscontent/ASJ/Acceleration_and_Resonance.pdf.

Calhoun, Adele Ahlberg. *Spiritual Disciplines Handbook: Practices that Transform Us.* Downers Grove, IL: InterVarsity, 2015.

Root, Andrew. *The Church after Innovation: Questioning Our Obsession with Work, Creativity, and Entrepreneurship.* Grand Rapids: Baker Academic, 2022.

———. *The Congregation in a Secular Age.* Grand Rapids: Baker Academic, 2021.

Rosa, Hartmut. "Available, Accessible, Attainable: The Mindset of Growth and the Resonance Conception of the Good Life." In *The Good Life Beyond Growth: New*

Perspectives, edited by Harmut Rosa and Christoph Henning, 39–54. New York: Routledge, 2018.

———. *Resonance: A Sociology of Our Relationship to the World*. Cambridge: Polity, 2019.

———. *The Uncontrollability of the World*. Cambridge: Polity, 2020.

Smith, James K. A. *How (Not) to Be Secular: Reading Charles Taylor*. Grand Rapids: Eerdmans, 2014.

Susen, Simon. "The Resonance of Resonance: Critical Theory as a Sociology of World Relations." *International Journal of Politics, Culture, and Society* 33.3 (2020) 309–44.

Taizé. "Taizé: Journeying Together." https://www.taize.fr/en.

7

Transitions Shaping Our Story and Identity
St. Paul's Catholic Parish

Joel Thiessen

INTRODUCTION

ST. PAUL'S IS A growing, multiethnic, forty-plus-year-old Catholic parish in an urban center in Western Canada.[1] Like many congregations, St. Paul's has experienced a series of transitions over its history that shape the stories it tells of itself and the subculture it aspires to. In this chapter, I chart six transitions that set the backdrop for three storylines at St. Paul's: (1) an emphasis on growth in numbers of parishioners, building space, and spiritual formation; (2) an emphasis on fostering a hospitable religious community; and (3) an emphasis on collective versus priestly ownership of parish ministry. Together, these changes and narratives inform a sense of "us" at St. Paul's. Throughout, I weave in sociological research, concepts, and analysis to help locate and interpret these transitions and storylines. Along the way I reflect on how the insights at St. Paul's might intersect with other congregations, Catholic or otherwise.

This material arises from data I gathered over a year-long period with two research assistants—Kennedy Quantz and Phillip Blindenbach—at St. Paul's, starting in July 2021. We interviewed nine leaders in total, including

1. All church and congregant names are pseudonyms to protect anonymity.

paid as well as lay volunteer leaders; participated in observational activities, including a facility tour, eight masses over multiple weekends, three Knights of Columbus gatherings, three Catholic Women's League meetings, two preparatory first Communion sessions, one rite of Christian initiation of adults (RCIA) meeting, and three confirmation classes; we surveyed 202 parishioners; led a half-day Appreciative Inquiry event with fifty-three highly involved leaders and members, who reflected on key periods and experiences in St. Paul's history; conducted a community demographics analysis of those who live within parish boundaries; and performed a content analysis on several sources, including St. Paul's website, bulletins, and historical records and data.

TRANSITIONS

Congregations change. As we've seen in many of the chapters already, some changes are intentional, while others are imposed. Some transformations are due to factors that a congregation controls, and others arise due to factors beyond a congregation's power. Congregational shifts intersect with the micro- (i.e., individuals), meso- (i.e., organizations like a church or denomination), and macro-system(s) (i.e., the societal environment beyond the congregation) that congregations are part of.[2] Regardless of the source or reason, change—including a group's responses and adaptations along the way—impacts a congregation's trajectory and the stories it tells of its past, present, and future. In the process, a congregation's subculture and identity evolve.

Over four decades, St. Paul's has navigated six transitions that influence the stories it tells today. Each transition ranges in scale, scope, and impact. The first was the end to twenty-five years of sharing a facility with a Protestant congregation. During this period each congregation had their own sanctuary, governance and finance structures, and personnel. They shared some common spaces and, at times, collaborated on joint ventures. Over time, the Catholic parish grew and the Protestant church diminished in size, which resulted in an end to this partnership. As one interviewee said, "In many ways, we overpowered. . . . It made it a difficult relationship because they felt dominated . . . with their congregation continuing to shrink and ours continuing to grow. It made sense for them to move out."

2. Ammerman et al., *Studying Congregations*; Parson and Leas, *Understanding Your Congregation*.

Shortly after, the second shift arose—another shared building arrangement, this time with a smaller Catholic parish. The smaller Catholic community was unsuccessful in its efforts to raise funds to build its own facility (they raised $500,000) and thus turned to St. Paul's to rent their second nave. This partnership soon evolved into an amalgamation between the two Catholic parishes (more on this merger shortly).

Third, the bishop assigned a new priest to St. Paul's, Fr. Bob. Fr. Bob is a dynamic and relational leader who has a clear sense of what he wants for parish life. He arrived on the heels of an unfruitful year-long tenure with the previous priest, who followed a much beloved priest beforehand who had served the parish for thirteen years. Fr. Bob was given a threefold mandate from the bishop: "First is put protocols in place, because people did their own stuff. . . . Secondly, to amalgamate two congregations into one. And third, . . . build a bigger building to accommodate the whole congregation." Fr. Bob was to introduce these changes immediately upon his arrival. Fr. Bob proceeded to oversee the merging of the two parishes. This included dissolving the two parish councils and forming a new one with members from both parishes, developing clearer systems and structures for operating the parish, and charting a vision forward for St. Paul's.

The amalgamation set the stage for the fourth critical transition, launching a multi-million-dollar renovation of St. Paul's that doubled the nave capacity to 1,200. The smaller Catholic parish that amalgamated with St. Paul's contributed the $500,000 it raised previously, providing a jump start to the $12.2 million fundraising campaign. The beautifully renovated building was completed just before the COVID-19 pandemic.

The pandemic marked the fifth change at St. Paul's. Provincial health restrictions were difficult in some ways for the parish. The diocese mandated that the parish lay off several staff, volunteer involvement diminished, youth became less involved, and concerns about paying for the newly renovated building along with basic operational costs were high. Still, St. Paul's adapted very quickly. Fr. Bob recounts offering "speed masses" in the initial weekends of the pandemic, where fifteen people attended, then cleaning occurred before the next fifteen people were welcomed, and so forth, throughout each day. Fr. Bob also purchased a camera and learned how to record and live stream masses (once restrictions ceased, so too did livestreaming masses at St. Paul's), and several midweek gatherings continued on Zoom, with higher-than-normal attendance in some cases. Throughout the months of public health restrictions, St. Paul's welcomed nearly 1,200 in-person attendees across six masses each weekend, with some indications of the pandemic deepening some people's faith. As with many congregations, it is too early to tell the longer-term effects of the pandemic on parishes like St. Paul's. This said, attentiveness to congregational adaptation and resilience will surely be storylines when assessing the full impact of the pandemic on congregations.

The sixth transition is that, following our time at St. Paul's, the bishop reassigned Fr. Bob to another parish, after serving for nine years. As will become clearer, Fr. Bob's visionary leadership was instrumental to many aspects of flourishing at St. Paul's. Like the pandemic, only time will tell if or what impact this leadership change will have on this parish.

Before turning to the stories told at St. Paul's, you might find it helpful to reflect upon the transitions in the life of your own congregation. What would you say are the key changes experienced before and after your involvement in this church? How, if at all, were different transitions related to one another? Were those shifts intentional or unintentional, guided internally or imposed from outside? How have those changes impacted congregational life, for better or worse, into who and what your church is today and could be tomorrow? How might the answers to these questions vary from different members' vantage points, past and present? In what way does your theological tradition inform how you frame these transitions? Questions such as these can be useful primers to orient a congregation to the stories it tells and potentially toward a church's flourishing.

STORYLINES

As we observed, interacted with, and listened to those at St. Paul's, three narratives rose to the surface. First, they emphasized numerical, building space, and spiritual growth. Second, they stressed being a hospitable religious community. Third, they spoke of collective versus priestly ownership of parish ministry.

Growth Mindset

We regularly observed a narrated link that numerical growth plus financial growth aides spiritual growth. Recalling the bishop's mandate to Fr. Bob to amalgamate two congregations and build a larger facility, we discovered that St. Paul's is the "largest parish in Western Canada," a fact subsequently mentioned with pride by many. Over four thousand attended one of six masses on a weekly basis before the pandemic. St. Paul's serves nearly eight thousand families within its parish boundaries. They attribute their growth to a combination of the merger with another Catholic parish (like St. Jerome's in chapter two), no nearby Catholic parish to compete with, and population growth in the suburbs fueled by immigration. As Fr. Bob told me, "I don't see any church being built here. So, it's going to grow.... This church is not going to be enough—with the amount of things that the church is[,] . . . the church has this potential, quite a bit!" Their central narrative is "build it and they will come." The reasons for growth remind us that sometimes contextual variables, or those factors beyond the control of a congregation, such as demographic changes or little "competition," are in play. In other words, congregational growth or decline is not strictly about what congregations do or do not do (e.g., preaching or programming), though these considerations certainly have an important role.[3]

We heard repeated refrains celebrating numerical growth, a reason for the needed multi-million dollar building renovation that ought to yield even more growth. We often encountered ideas that the renovations are "something to help [us] welcome more people" and to leave a "legacy." Still, many are concerned about carrying a $12 million, thirty-five-year mortgage. One member of the finance council noted, "I don't think we have a lot of extra money . . . for programming." The pandemic exacerbated these financial challenges. As such, there is a steady stream of appeals for donations to pay down the debt. For example, in St. Paul's welcome video, parishioners are encouraged to "buy God a cup of coffee every day toward the donor wall. . . . Isn't God worth it?" In another appeal video, parishioners are told, "We are making progress on this thirty-five-year mortgage, *but we believe that we can do better*" (emphasis added). The goal is to pay the mortgage down in twenty years, which would save $5 million in interest, "money that can be put toward ministry works, sacramental programs, and supporting the spiritual needs of our 7,600 families." These reflections remind us that growth can have its downsides, introducing what sociologists refer to as "organizational strain" or the "discrepancy between organizational demands and organizational capacity."[4]

---

3. Ammerman et al., *Studying Congregations*; Hoge and Roozen, *Understanding Church Growth*.

4. Haas and Drabek, *Complex Organizations*, 251.

As much as we heard about the excitement surrounding numeric growth, Fr. Bob is quick to note that "we're not interested in numbers, we are interested in quality." Namely, spiritual formation and growth is the aim of numerical and financial growth; the renovated building is a powerful cultural symbol that signifies "a place for communing with God." As one interviewee articulated, "in order to grow as a parish, . . . everything we do at St. Paul's needs to lead us back to God."

We asked many at St. Paul's where they would like to see the parish in five years. Many spoke about continued numerical growth, reduced debt, and ongoing spiritual growth. These responses signal central elements, some of which are presently a reality and others that remain an ideal—at times with a sizeable gap between the two—to St. Paul's story, identity, and subculture.

Hospitable Community

Many we interacted with described St. Paul's as "a welcoming parish." And yet, we heard often that St. Paul's has not always been perceived this way. Several interviewees noted that during the two facility partnerships there was some observed rivalry between the different churches, competition among subgroups within the same parish, and varying levels of receptivity to different priests. As Fr. Bob said, "St. Paul's . . . didn't have a great reputation. . . . [I] didn't feel welcomed as a priest, because I was in the neighboring parishes too. . . . When I used to come here . . . it was kind of a different attitude. . . . I don't think many of us [priests] were interested in landing here."

The following interviewee makes this observation on Fr. Bob's impact at St. Paul's following the amalgamation with the second Catholic parish: "There has always been a welcomeness, but it used to be a divided welcomeness. . . . It's a very diverse community. . . . Fr. Bob's done a good job making sure it's blended." This interviewee provided an example, mentioning "something called a cultural day and basically it was who could cook their best food. And it was a competition." Fr. Bob let us know that "competition" language was eventually dropped, to ensure "our focus is on the LORD and let's keep it there."

Today, "hospitable community," "family," and "home" are descriptors that parishioners use to characterize St. Paul's. For example, one interviewee said, "I've been involved in many parishes. And one of the things that I say about St. Paul's is it has a very welcoming spirit." Our research team experienced this hospitality throughout our time at St. Paul's. Part of this gradual shift can be attributed to leadership, starting with the bishop's mandate and support for Fr. Bob to amalgamate the two parishes, and then Fr. Bob's ability to progressively influence the congregational culture over time. Collective ownership and involvement in parish activities is another central factor, which I return to later.

St. Paul's reported transformation in this area calls our attention to "flourishing" as a fluid and dynamic rather than a static concept. Congregations that are flourishing do not flourish in all areas nor does an area of flourishing or floundering remain indefinitely. Congregations ebb and flow through different stages of the life cycle of a congregation,[5] a finding that might provide hope to congregations currently struggling in one or more area and caution to those presently thriving.

As St. Paul's frames its story around a hospitable community, this account is complicated and strained relative to its growth narrative. Growth has had unintended consequences for St. Paul's being a hospitable community. Sociologists note that as church size grows, people's level of social embeddedness tends to diminish; it is more difficult to know others or to ensure group conformity.[6] This reality is magnified in Catholic versus Protestant contexts where there are fewer parishes and priests relative to the number of people who say they are Catholic.[7] One way we witnessed this tension was during rites of passage rituals, all prior to Fr. Bob's transition. When attending services over multiple weekends, we were struck by how impersonal—almost factory-like—the sacrament of reconciliation or first Communion could be experienced for those families involved. We observed many families stand when called upon, priests read scripts without looking up and out to those they were speaking to, and visiting priests to this parish declare, "*We as a parish* are praying for you" (emphasis added). There was also one occasion where a priest invited all families present for a family member's first Communion to stand and then proceeded to read the scripted material—only that no families were present in that mass who stood for that occasion. These observations remind us that congregations can tell stories or build a subculture around areas (e.g., growth) that sometimes add organizational strain to other areas (e.g., hospitable community).

5. Saarinen, *Life Cycle*.
6. Eagle, "Negative Relationship"; Stroope, "Social Networks."
7. Bibby, *Restless Churches*, 135.

Collective Ownership

Reinforcing a hospitable community ethos, one of Fr. Bob's core tenets is that "the parish does not belong to the priests; it belongs to the parishioners." He put this cultural value into practice shortly after arriving at St. Paul's. He disbanded and then reestablished the various leadership councils, including members from both Catholic parishes that amalgamated. One longtime member recalls the goal to "bring them [the other Catholic parish] back to St. Paul's and make them feel welcome, get them participating on committees and . . . feeling a part of it. . . . It was important we welcomed them and . . . found a way they could come into the community." Many at St. Paul's also spoke favorably of the emphasis on including, collaborating with, equipping, and empowering others in leadership. We heard several stories involving parishioners being invited into leadership, or where congregants had ideas for new ministry initiatives and Fr. Bob or other leaders encouraged them to "go for it." This is partially reflected in St. Paul's strong subculture of volunteerism—for instance, over one thousand parishioners volunteered pre-pandemic.

As our data collection continued it became clearer that Fr. Bob was instrumental to St. Paul's flourishing. One parishioner noted they were "grateful for the stability of the parish over the last few years; no movement of priests has been positive for that stability." Yet, as another told us, "We all know priests are only expected to be here three to five years. . . . That's the norm." With no foreknowledge of his pending transition, we probed the anticipated impact should Fr. Bob transition from St. Paul's. One response, typical of others, suggested, "I don't think it's gonna make a huge impact . . . because of everything that he's putting in place." By this the interviewee meant intentional efforts to include many people in the shared ministry of the parish.

This statement also refers to systems and structures that Fr. Bob instituted, reflective of the first mandate given to him from the bishop at his appointment: "Put protocols in place, because people did their own stuff." We learned about "the binder" that stored parish policies and procedures. For example, the binder is integral to volunteer activities: "When you have procedures in place, people know what their expectations are. . . . With all our volunteers, there's training manuals, there's position descriptions, there's charts for different ministries, everybody is given what the expectations are for whatever they're doing. . . . I think when you let people know what . . . you expect of them, then people don't want to disappoint." Studies of organizations suggest that this type of clarity can be instrumental to helping an organization intentionally and meaningfully live into its core reason for existence.[8] Put differently, organizations rarely flourish by accident; intentional systems and structures are paramount.

When asked what impact he thinks his eventual departure would have on St. Paul's, Fr. Bob said the following:

> The moment I go, I want to be forgotten. And I mean it. . . . It's not about me. . . . When I'm gone, I want the parish to function seamlessly. . . . That's the greatest gift they could give me. . . . If they could just function on their own and smooth. . . . I don't want them to miss me in a way that, like, 'Uh, now what?' . . . *We* build the parish. . . . *We* built the building. . . . *We* are the church. (Emphasis original.)

Research suggests the potential impact of leadership change in Catholic parishes might be lower than in other religious contexts because of the emphasis on tradition, structure, liturgy, and a shared Catholic subculture rather than the individual persona of a single leader.[9] Still, research in other congregational contexts documents that leadership changes can significantly shape a congregation, especially if a leader was pivotal to that group's flourishing.[10] We will need to keep the tape rolling at St. Paul's to assess the impact of this leadership change.

ST. PAUL'S AND YOUR CONGREGATION

You might rightly ask, how do the distinctive experiences at St. Paul's help our congregation? After all, St. Paul's is of another theological tradition or numerical size or has markedly different transitions and storylines than our church. While these variations might be true, social scientific analysis of congregations points to many common elements across diverse church contexts. I want to suggest five lines of analysis at St. Paul's that, if you pay close attention, could yield important insights for local ministry in your context.

First, the stories congregations tell can speak to *both* reality and aspiration. As Galen Watts expresses, "Telling one's story is not merely descriptive, but also *prescriptive*."[11] Stories partially function to direct a congregation to

---

8. Drucker, *Managing the Nonprofit*; Lockyer, *Finding Our Way*.
9. Gallagher, "Continuity and Community."
10. Schuurman, *Subversive Evangelical*; Mulder and Marti, *Glass Church*.
11. Watts, *Spiritual Turn*, 153 (emphasis original).

embody an ideal identity they wish to live into. At St. Paul's, being a hospitable community where the laity collectively own the vision and activities captures the experiences of some leaders and members. Yet, as noted, St. Paul's confronts some challenges to be a hospitable community relative to its larger size. This is not to suggest that just because a church is large it cannot be a hospitable community. Nevertheless, Fr. Bob and other lay leaders keep these narratives front of mind in the parish to encourage members toward these desired ends. Doing so makes sense, as it reinforces central identity markers that set "us," our congregation, apart from the church up the road.

One aspect to a flourishing congregation is identity clarity, knowing where a church has come from, currently is, and is going.[12] Churches with identity clarity ensure that the decisions made, activities pursued, and symbols and meanings held aid a congregation's ability to fulfil its vision and mission. In this regard, organizations often live in the tension between reality and aspiration. Tying identity to the stories congregations tell, James Hopewell says that narratives function for people to "give sense and order to their lives."[13] He goes on to state that the "experience of the lived present must have a narrative character, because it necessarily ties the perception of the moment to the memory of past events and to the anticipation of the future."[14]

Linking these observations and analyses to your context, what is distinctive about your congregation's subculture and what are the aspirational ideals that your faith community is drawn toward? How closely do those intentions match current realities? Who in your faith community has contributed to these aims, and who has been on the sidelines? How does your theological tradition, church's history and transitions, demographic composition, leader makeup, or governance structure and decisions influence the stories your congregation tells in these directions?

Second, congregational stories reflect a confluence of institutional and contextual factors. These include individual, leader, organizational, and denominational histories, perceptions, and experiences, alongside societal and demographic changes beyond the congregation. Together, these factors contributed to a clear-cut subculture at St. Paul's that evolved as its leaders and members as well as the surrounding social environment changed. Past research suggests that growing congregations tend to attribute their growth to things they did (i.e., institutional factors), while churches diminishing

---

12. Hopewell, *Congregation*; Ammerman et al., *Studying Congregations*.
13. Hopewell, *Congregation*, 5.
14. Hopewell, *Congregation*, 47.

in size tend to explain their losses by pointing to things beyond their control (i.e., contextual factors).[15] The truth likely exists between these two accounts. Congregations would be wise to pay careful attention and accurately and objectively assess those factors in their setting. Still, how congregations perceive and frame these stories, however accurate or inaccurate, impacts the emerging subculture of a congregation. The question becomes how do the stories your church tells about itself, the ways they are told, and who tells them shape who your congregation is becoming in light of your church's past and current experiences and perceptions?

Third, well-intentioned narratives and steps toward congregational flourishing can simultaneously introduce or amplify organizational strain in other areas. This was the case with some of the financial pressures plus less personable elements (i.e., recall the earlier story of the sacrament of reconciliation or first Communion) in the face of a growing St. Paul's parish. Organizational strain does not mean that a congregation should necessarily avoid pursuing certain goals, only that a church needs to also be attentive to the possible drawbacks and associated responses in the process. Importantly, a congregation must weigh the pros and cons of organizational strain relative to its ability to fulfil what it believes to be core to its subculture and identity.

Adaptability, to be resilient in the face of strain, is a valuable trait for organizations. Vogus and Sutcliffe say that "resilience results from processes and dynamics that create or retain resources (cognitive, emotional, relational, or structural) in a form sufficiently flexible, storable, convertible, and malleable that enables organizations to successfully cope with and learn from the unexpected."[16] As one example, St. Paul's demonstrated its agility in response to pandemic lockdowns, driven largely from Fr. Bob's visionary leadership. Adaptability in one aspect of congregational life does not mean that a church is flexible in other areas, though I suspect this is often the case. Research indicates that flourishing organizations tend to be highly adaptable and innovative.[17] Agility and resilience are part of the core fabric and stories in a congregation, as demonstrated in several of the case studies in this book.

Fourth, part of what binds St. Paul's storylines together, and possibly helps to explain areas of flourishing at St. Paul's, is collective ownership.

---

15. McMullin, "Secularization of Sunday"; Flatt et al., "Secularization and Attribution."

16. Vogus and Sutcliffe, "Organizational Resilience," 3419.

17. Christerson and Flory, *Rise*; Schuurman, *Subversive Evangelical*; Mulder and Marti, *Glass Church*.

This approach invites people into a shared story and equips and empowers many to contribute to the evolving story and to own the parish's story for themselves. This quest is aided when one experiences a hospitable community, with the likely by-product of numerical, financial, and spiritual growth at the parish. The renovated building represents a foundational symbol of these identity markers at St. Paul's.

Building on research at the Fuller Youth Institute on "keychain leadership," leadership development and lay involvement is critical for congregational life.[18] These dynamics are particularly important in Catholic settings where the paid clergy to parishioner ratio is much lower than in Protestant contexts. Therefore, Catholic parishes are especially dependent upon the ministry of the laity, though this need is not exclusive to Catholics. One caution for denominations and congregations is to avoid allowing denominational leaders, clergy, or even lay leaders to get in the way of equipping and empowering the ministry of the laity.[19]

As you think about your congregation, how would you assess leadership development and lay involvement? Who holds the leadership keys in your church and how (un)willing are they to share those keys with others? Who or what would need to change in your church to become more open and effective in developing new leaders, and how might doing so strengthen your congregation's capacity to flourish? What narratives are held in front of your congregants that would compel them to pursue deeper engagement in congregational life? How do your congregation's theological beliefs, rituals, and values inform these stories and approaches? The reflections and implied actions that arise from these and related questions have the potential to broaden the base of those who take hold of your congregation's story, for those people to encourage others to do likewise, and to inspire the congregation to collectively move in unison as a church to exemplify the desired subculture and identity of this congregation.

Fifth, the stories and associated functions and flourishing that arose at St. Paul's were unlikely to occur without Fr. Bob's leadership. This includes the combination of (1) the bishop's threefold mandate for Fr. Bob to establish systems and structures, amalgamate two parishes, and build a larger facility; (2) the bishop's unwavering support for Fr. Bob to do some of this difficult work; and (3) Fr. Bob's priestly authoritative presence that combined a warm and personable demeanor with a clear set of convictions on how things

18. Griffin et al., *Growing Young*, 50–87.
19. McAlpine et al., "Are You Listening?"

should be done at the parish. As we have seen in several of our case studies across Canada, visionary leadership appears to be a necessary but not sufficient contributor to congregational flourishing. That is, leadership alone cannot determine a church's trajectory, but leadership can have a significant impact. In some respects, the stories that congregations tell and embody in the fiber of their being, and ultimately their flourishing as a community of faith, rise and fall upon their leaders and the tone and subculture they set.

I do not have space to go into the following in detail, but there is much discussion across theological traditions and congregations on how best to raise leaders for today and tomorrow—notably, with a smaller pipeline of clergy on the horizon. Should this development occur through formal educational institutions or in-house within congregations? What are the skills and traits that clergy need, from theological instruction to deep spiritual formation roots themselves, to pastoral care capacities, organizational acumen, cultural exegesis abilities, communication skills, and so forth?[20] I cannot underscore the following strongly enough—the strength of congregations will in large part rise and fall based on its leaders and their ability to do all the things noted above and more. As has long been the case, careful and structured clergy development and mentoring will be essential for congregations moving forward.

CONCLUSION

I close with the following statement made by a parishioner when asked to summarize what is working at St. Paul's to help it flourish. This statement was met by applause by the fifty-plus people gathered at the Appreciative Inquiry event: "We are a diverse and welcoming sacramental, multicultural Catholic community focused on learning (formation), evangelization, and volunteering, with great leadership, meeting in a wonderful building, and worshipping, all for the Glory of God!" This pronouncement captures the three central storylines at St. Paul's—growth in its many forms, hospitality, and collective ownership. For a parishioner to articulate these things so clearly is indicative of how deeply St. Paul's subcultural narratives of "us" are embedded in this parish. Importantly, these narratives reflect a storied history of change and transition, with the rest of the story still to unfold for St. Paul's.

---

20. McAlpine et al., "Are You Listening?"

QUESTIONS FOR REFLECTION

1. What transitions has your congregation experienced, and how have those changes impacted congregational life, for better or worse, with regard to who and what your church is today and could be tomorrow?

2. What is distinctive about your congregation's subculture, what are the aspirational ideals that your faith community is drawn toward, and how closely do those intentions match current realities?

3. How does your congregation's theological tradition, history and transitions, demographic composition, leader makeup, or governance structure and decisions influence the stories your congregation tells of itself?

4. Who holds the leadership keys in your church and how (un)willing are they to share those keys with others? Who or what would need to change in your church to become more open and effective in developing new leaders, and how might doing so strengthen your congregation's capacity to flourish?

BIBLIOGRAPHY

Ammerman, Nancy T., et al., eds. *Studying Congregations: A New Handbook.* Nashville: Abingdon, 1998.

Bibby, Reginald. *Restless Churches: How Canada's Churches Can Contribute to the Emerging Religious Renaissance.* Ottawa, ON: Wood Lake, 2004.

Christerson, Brad, and Richard Flory. *The Rise of Network Christianity: How Independent Leaders Are Changing the Religious Landscape.* New York: Oxford University Press, 2017.

Drucker, Peter F. *Managing the Nonprofit Organization: Principles and Practices.* New York: HarperCollins, 2006.

Eagle, David. "The Negative Relationship between Size and the Probability of Weekly Attendance in Churches in the United States." *Socius* 2 (2016) 1–10.

Flatt, Kevin, et al. "Secularization and Attribution: How Mainline Protestant Clergy and Congregants Explain Church Growth and Decline." *Sociology of Religion* 79 (2018) 78–107.

Gallagher, Sally K. "Continuity and Community: An Analysis of Membership Turnover, Growth and Decline in Three Congregations." *Review of Religious Research* 62 (2020) 333–49.

Griffin, Brad, et al. *Growing Young: Six Essential Strategies to Help Young People Discover and Love Your Church.* Grand Rapids: Baker, 2016.

Haas, J. Eugene, and Thomas E. Drabek. *Complex Organizations: A Sociological Perspective.* New York: Macmillan, 1973.

Hoge, Dean A., and David A. Roozen, eds. *Understanding Church Growth and Decline: 1950–1978.* New York: Pilgrim, 1979.

Hopewell, James F. *Congregation: Stories and Structures.* Philadelphia: Fortress Press, 1987.

Lockyer, Jeff. *Finding Our Way: Reclaiming the First-Century Church in the Twenty-First Century.* Eugene, OR: Wipf & Stock, 2021.

McAlpine, Bill, et al. "Are You Listening? The Relevance of What Pastoral/Denominational Leaders and Theological Educators Are Saying about Preparing Leaders for Ministry." *Practical Theology* 12 (2019) 415–32.

McMullin, Steve. "The Secularization of Sunday: Real or Perceived Competition for Churches." *Review of Religious Research* 55 (2013) 43–59.

Mulder, Mark T., and Gerardo Marti. *The Glass Church: Robert H. Schuller, the Crystal Cathedral, and the Strain of Megachurch Ministry.* Chicago: Rutgers University Press, 2020.

Parson, George, and Speed B. Leas. *Understanding Your Congregation as a System.* Lanham, MD: Rowman & Littlefield, 1993.

Saarinen, Martin F. *The Life Cycle of a Congregation.* Herndon, VA: Alban Institute, 1986.

Schuurman, Peter J. *The Subversive Evangelical: The Ironic Charisma of an Irreligious Megachurch.* Advancing Studies in Religion 6. Montreal: McGill-Queen's University Press, 2019.

Stroope, Samuel. "Social Networks and Religion: The Role of Congregational Social Embeddedness in Religious Belief and Practice." *Sociology of Religion* 73 (2012) 273–98.

Vogus, Timothy J., and Kathleen M. Sutcliffe. "Organizational Resilience: Towards a Theory and Research Agenda." 2007 IEEE International Conference on Systems, Man and Cybernetics, Montreal (Oct. 2007) 3418–22. doi: 10.1109/ICSMC.2007.4414160.

Watts, Galen. *The Spiritual Turn: The Religion of the Heart and the Making of Romantic Liberal Modernity.* New York: Oxford University Press, 2022.

8

Caring about Ascension Cares
A Profile of a Parish-Based Community Outreach Program

Bernardine Ketelaars and Fr. Robert Weaver

INTRODUCTION

FOLLOWING JESUS' GLORIOUS RESURRECTION, he instructed his disciples to "go therefore and make disciples of all nations" (Matt 28:19 NRSVCE). Since then, Christians have embarked on this Great Commission in a multitude of ways. In this chapter we highlight and elaborate on how Ascension Church, a Roman Catholic church located in an urban setting within Central Canada, is uniquely and effectively implementing Jesus' instructions.[1] More specifically, Ascension Church is doing this by clearly manifesting two key aspects of the outward dimension of the flourishing congregations construct—neighborhood involvement and evangelism.[2]

Neighborhood involvement is characterized by a church or faith community, through its activities, demonstrating a tangible presence within its immediate environment to such an extent that even nonmembers would

---

1. In order to protect the anonymity of program patrons and parish staff and members, we used the pseudonym Fr. Stanley as well as pseudonyms for other pastoral team members and program patrons.

2. McAlpine et al., *Signs of Life*, 17.

notice if it were no longer there.[3] As for evangelism, this can be considered efforts undertook by religious group members to attract other individuals to the group so they adhere to similar beliefs and behaviors.[4] For Christians, this is centered on inviting others to have a personal and ongoing relationship with Jesus Christ. And for Catholic-Christians, a strong emphasis is placed on nourishing and strengthening this personal relationship with Jesus through active participation in the church, which includes attending mass and receiving the Eucharist. So, for Catholics, the aim of evangelism includes, somewhere along the line, inviting non-Catholics to become Catholic.

We can attest to Ascension Church's unique and effective forms of neighborhood involvement and evangelism because of our case study of this congregation, which we outline and explain in considerable detail in this chapter. At this point, we invite you to consider the way(s) in which your own congregation is involved in its surrounding neighborhood as well as its evangelistic activities. By doing this, you can compare and contrast your congregation with our case study of Ascension Church. And now we will "set the stage" for our case study description by highlighting some key historical and contextual information pertaining to Ascension Church.

SETTING THE STAGE

As we mentioned, Ascension Church is situated in an urban setting within central Canada. It is an architecturally impressive structure and is rightfully considered historically significant, as the first mass was celebrated there prior to Confederation. In 2014, the church was closed for regular use due to the need for a new heating system as well as repairs to the roof. This prompted an intensive fundraising project; the church was reopened for public use in 2019.[5]

Approximately 19,000 people live within Ascension Church's parish boundaries and their average age is about forty-eight years old. Just over 45 percent of the region's residents have never been married, while 27.7 percent are married. Nearly 44 percent of the households are deemed low income. Child poverty rates are even higher, as 61.3 percent of children aged zero to five years old live in low-income households as do 53.9 percent

---

3. McAlpine et al., *Signs of Life*, 17.
4. McAlpine et al., *Signs of Life*, 200–201.
5. Interview with Fr. Stanley, Mar. 17, 2022.

of six- to seventeen-year-olds. In terms of religious affiliation, almost 70 percent (69.2) of the region's residents are Christian, 20 percent claim no religious affiliation, while 6.9 percent are Muslim. Less than 4 percent are Hindu, Buddhist, Sikh, Jewish, or another religion.[6]

Ascension Church, like most Roman Catholic churches within the diocese it is situated in, as well as throughout Canada and North America, has witnessed a steady decline in mass attendance. A Canada-wide, post-pandemic Angus Reid Survey was completed in 2022 between January 21 and April 7. It found that, on average, 14 percent of Roman Catholics attend Mass once or twice a month.[7] However, in 2016, as reported in the program proposal outlined below, Ascension Church reported that only 7.5 percent of the Roman Catholics living within its parish boundaries were attending Mass at least once a month—just over half of the national average of 14 percent.

Around this time the leadership of Ascension Church, cognizant that they served a region inhabited by a high proportion of low-income residents facing various challenges, recognized the importance of being more visible within the broader community and so they began to plan accordingly. In doing so they were, perhaps unwittingly, preparing to implement a highly significant indicator of outward dimension—neighborhood involvement.[8]

In September 2018, Ascension Church's pastoral team began preparing a proposal for a church-based outreach program. After some revisions and updating of information, the "Proposal for a Comprehensive Outreach Program at Ascension Parish" was completed in December 2018. This proposal included information on Ascension Church as well as key demographic information pertaining to the population within its parish boundaries, a proposed budget for 2019–22, and specific program goals. These goals included assisting individuals and families in need, increasing awareness of Ascension Church within its parish boundaries, and encouraging the formation of intentional disciples of Jesus Christ. It also stated that the program would be known as Ascension Cares.

One of the things the proposal called for was a needs assessment to help the team identify what forms of outreach were needed and, of these, which ones had the greatest priority. We were impressed at how the leadership of Ascension Cares did not presume to know the needs of those who

---

6. Statistics Canada, "2016 Census."
7. Angus Reid Institute and Cardus, "Religious Spectrum."
8. McAlpine et al., *Signs of Life*, 17.

lived within the parish boundaries without first conducting a formal needs assessment that included community input.

Deacon Patrick, one of the original architects of Ascension Cares, explained the needs assessment was conducted by developing a survey-type form that listed a large variety of potential services organized into different categories. It asked people to indicate the services they would find particularly beneficial as well other relevant ideas they had. The survey was circulated throughout Ascension parish but also at other strategic locations, such as schools, community centers, and retail establishments. The completed surveys were analyzed by calculating the number of times each potential service was selected and then determining its percentage of the total responses in each category. The top four or five activities in each category were considered for implementation.[9]

From this assessment the team envisioned program services being divided into three distinct yet related categories. These categories were: (1) support/education; (2) physical exercise/relaxation; and (3) socializing/fun. Later in this chapter we provide examples of different programs, all under the umbrella of Ascension Cares, that belong to one of these categories.

The fact that the needs assessment results contributed to the development and implementation of actual programs speaks to the dedication of the Ascension Cares team and the worth of conducting such an initiative. Has your congregation's leadership team ever conducted a needs assessment? If so, did its results translate into actual services or programs? If so, how come? If not, why not?

The vision statement of Ascension Church emphasizes the importance of members being like beacons of light who are service-oriented and merciful disciples of Jesus Christ. As Deacon Patrick pointed out, this vision statement is aligned with a congregation that has a conspicuous presence within the surrounding community with lots of emphasis on mercy, service, and discipleship. The deacon's insight is indicative of a clear sense of self-identity that characterizes a flourishing congregation, in which members, including leaders, convey a sense of direction and conviction.[10]

As Ascension's pastoral team navigated through the multitude of challenges that emerged during the pandemic, the launching of Ascension Cares demonstrated they were ready and able to put their parish vision statement into action. And we were ready and able to hear their story.

---

9. Deacon, email message with attachment to researchers, June 26, 2023.
10. McAlpine et al., *Signs of Life*, 20.

CASE STUDY

In September 2021, we invited Ascension parish's pastoral team to participate in a case study that would include interviews and the administration of a questionnaire. Through this invitation, they were asked to consider two things: (1) taking part in the Flourishing Congregations Institute nationwide study with an emphasis on Ascension Cares and (2) whether they would fit the description of a "flourishing congregation"—specifically, to ask themselves, "Would our neighborhood notice if our church was no longer here?" The latter question is based on the notion of neighborhood involvement that we highlighted earlier. We were delighted when Fr. Stanley, administrator of Ascension parish, accepted our invitation.

Service-Oriented Evangelization

In April 2022, we conducted a group interview, via Zoom, with several members of the pastoral team. These were Fr. Stanley, Deacon Patrick, Joan (the pastoral minister), Linda (the outreach coordinator), and Janice (the youth and family minister).

The interview yielded some important highlights related to what it means to be a flourishing congregation; this includes recognizing that outreach and evangelism extend beyond the church doors with the intent of touching the lives of all within the parish boundaries—not just Roman Catholics. Considering the steady decline in mass attendance we highlighted earlier, it is vital that Catholic churches make a concerted effort to be a visible and uplifting presence to people from various faith backgrounds, as well as those with no faith. Consequently, it was wonderful to hear the Ascension team discuss how their outreach efforts would grow as pandemic restrictions were loosening.

Deacon Patrick explained how the onset of COVID-19 prompted the parish to live stream all their masses and this led to an ongoing and vibrant social media presence. He noted their Facebook presence has 2,700 likes, their YouTube presence has 1,900 followers, and their Instagram account Ascension Cares also has an online presence with 800 followers. Furthermore, the parish website has an "Ask me anything" option with 700 followers.

Linda explained how through Ascension Cares the team offers various services for people living in the area, including people living in poverty.

These services align with the three categories of services we outlined above. For instance, in the area of support/education, the Bountiful Basket program regularly provides fresh vegetables; clothing is typically distributed Friday mornings through the Help Yourself program. As for physical exercise/relaxation, a fitness class is provided. And for socializing/fun, there is a weekly community meal, a baking club, and opportunities to play cards and other games. As Linda stated, "Through [Ascension Cares] we engage with people, and they ask us questions, some even ask questions about the weekend masses. This becomes a form of evangelization. Through outreach, we support people when they need help."

Deacon Patrick also highlighted how many of the Ascension Cares programs are not explicitly religious, but they still have an evangelizing component as they lead people to ask, "Why are they doing this? And, Why do they give so freely?" As he noted, "Actions speak louder than words and with Ascension Cares we are showing what the church is about."

Indeed, the Ascension Cares team demonstrates different ways to "be church" by feeding, clothing, and caring for those in need. This is a congregation with members who live out the gospel message by responding to Jesus' great commandment—"just as I have loved you, you also should love one another" (John 13:34 NRSVCE). Jesus reminds us that whatever we do to one of these, our brothers and sisters, we do to him (cf. Matt 25:40). Clearly, Ascension Cares is a manifestation of Jesus' love for those struggling with poverty, poor health, and social isolation, and in doing so, invites others to love him back.

A Similar Story

We find this notion of church-based social programs having the potential to be evangelistic a fascinating one and we are not alone in this interest. For example, Ravi Gokani interviewed clients of Canadian Evangelical faith-based organizations (FBOs) that deliver social services and discovered some very interesting trends. For example, some clients were already practicing Christians before they came to the FBO, but their faith was strengthened as a result of receiving services. The author also reports that two clients, who considered themselves moderate Catholics, expressed a deepening of their belief in God.

Moreover, there were some other clients who stated they were not Christians, but they experienced an openness to the faith they did not have prior to receiving services, as they genuinely appreciated the concern and kindness demonstrated by service providers. And there were instances of clients with non-Christian perspectives, such as Buddhists, atheists, and agnostics, who became Christians during the time they received services.[11]

These findings from Gokani's study suggest that church-based social services, including those offered through Ascension Cares, have the potential to be evangelistic. It is not solely the services themselves that lead people to Christ but when people are prayerfully serving others as a form of discipleship, as does the Ascension Cares pastoral team, it can result in at least some of the patrons/clients being spiritually nourished and transformed. We noticed how our interview with the team helped members reflect on the fruitful nature of their grace-filled ministries. In fact, one member mentioned the need to do such reflections and/or interviews more often!

Growth and Formation

In July 2022, we conducted another interview with the Ascension Cares team, this time only with Linda and Deacon Patrick. During this interview, we heard about the origins of Ascension Cares and its plethora of community-based programs, and we indirectly met some of the people served by Ascension Cares through the stories told by Linda and Deacon Patrick. Through this interview, we also learned more about the nonjudgmental and evangelizing nature of Ascension Cares—some might view these terms as contradictory, but the work of Ascension Cares demonstrates otherwise. Indeed, those who serve the patrons of Ascension Cares are spreading the good news. This is evinced by Linda's comments:

> I think . . . [Ascension Cares] is true evangelization because . . . [we] are doing Jesus' work. When we are giving out bread, we are not asking for anything. If you need one or two loaves, if you have a big family, I am not going to question you; that is not our purpose. Our purpose is to be there and to serve the people who come to us the best we can. . . . It is not my job to question. Jesus did not question, he just did. And that's what I am trying to live[,] . . . to give freely without question or judgment and try to be an intentional disciple [of Christ Jesus]. Just doing the work, which is fulfilling. At the end of the week, I can look back and say, we did a lot of good work, and thank God for the opportunity to help people.

11. Gokani, "Client Transformation," 569.

Linda's statement about thanking God for the opportunity to help people reveals how God's grace illumines the attitude of the Ascension Cares team members and fuels their activities. This was made further evident by Deacon Patrick's explanation:

> There are two points: the diocesan rule of baptism is if someone comes to request a baptism, that is evidence of faith. If someone comes and asks for food, that is not an easy thing for people to do. If they do that, it is good enough. We want them to come and tell us what their need is, and we will help them. . . . A member of [the Society of] St. Vincent de Paul gave us a talk and said, If you start to feel they are cheating you, you are not looking at it in the right way because the deal is not between you and them, the deal is between you and God and God and them; they are never cheating you.

Another very fruitful and unique aspect of this outreach initiative is the number of patrons who, in turn, volunteer through Ascension Cares. One such patron, who also volunteered when her health permitted, is Nicole. While taking part in the exercise program, Nicole also assisted with community dinners. She shared that "sometimes you see familiar faces when you are involved with different things there because it is in our own community. So, I really enjoy coming here and getting together with other people and having a fun time."

This not-uncommon phenomenon of patrons becoming volunteers and serving others speaks to another way in which Ascension parish can be considered a flourishing congregation—its proclivity for forming disciples. Congregations are called to cultivate people's relationship with Jesus and help them live out his will in their lives.[12] Nicole is just one example of others who encountered Jesus through Ascension Cares, which led to their becoming volunteers and sharing his love with others. In other words, Ascension Cares is actively forming disciples of Christ Jesus.

In another example of how Ascension Cares is forming disciples, Linda explained that on various occasions she reaches out to local university students to volunteer; there are two post-secondary institutions within the parish's boundaries. She described these recruiting efforts as successful, as students are often willing to offer their services; they like to see and contribute toward charity in action. We propose that this service can also result in different students encountering the LORD Jesus and becoming Catholic.

---

12. McAlpine et al., *Signs of Life*, 96.

Given how much planning went into the creation of Ascension Cares, it is not surprising that the team closely monitors the number of people who access their services, and their records show a fairly steady increase in clientele. For instance, in July 2022 there were 1,883 recorded people who accessed at least one service; this number increased to 2,219 in November 2023. (It should be noted that these numbers are somewhat inflated since people who accessed two or more services would be counted two or more times.) Of all the services offered through Ascension Cares, the most accessed were Bountiful Basket, Help Yourself, and the community meal. Clearly, helping people meet their basic needs of nutrition, clothing, and socializing in a Christ-like, generous manner is a core aspect of Ascension Cares' neighborhood involvement.

A Closer Look at Bountiful Basket

Due to the high proportion of Ascension Cares patrons who access food through Bountiful Basket, in September 2022 we invited these patrons to fill out a questionnaire aimed at capturing some of their perceptions of the program. From this we gleaned some important insights. For instance, when asked about how often they accessed food from the Bountiful Basket program for the six-month period leading up to the day they completed the questionnaire, nearly 60 percent of the respondents stated, "quite often" (about two or three times per month) or "regularly" (every week or nearly every week). Moreover, when respondents considered if the Bountiful Basket program has led to their being better able to provide nutritious food for people in their household, almost two-thirds (about 62 percent) strongly agreed with this statement and approximately 31 percent agreed with it.

It is important to note that the Bountiful Basket program is not limited to helping people meet their nutritional needs, for it impacts the psychosocial realm as well. Over half (54.5 percent) of the respondents strongly agreed with a statement indicating that Bountiful Basket helped them feel closer to people within their neighborhood and 25 percent agreed with it. The program's impact is made even more apparent when we consider the comments of our research assistant, Donna Sousa, who noted the following interaction when observing a couple of patrons:

> Two university students came to pick up vegetables. They were new to the . . . area and came to [Bountiful Basket] only twice. They spoke with [Linda] and she invited them to the community

meal. Both appeared to be excited and said, "This would be a great opportunity to meet people from this area." This speaks to the multilevel of support that is offered through [Ascension Cares].[13]

Listening to Some Patrons

We wanted to hear more from some of the patrons of Ascension Cares and Linda generously arranged to have three patrons speak with us via Zoom. These interviews proved to be very rich and insightful.

For example, we were very much touched by the comments made by Judy, an eighty-one year old widow who volunteers at the community dinners. Judy emphasized how close-knit the community dinner patrons had become and said,

> A couple of weeks ago, one man did not show up. I knew that two days later he would be at another church. So, I had to go there and try to find him and wanted to make sure he was alright. You become attached to these people after a while.

When asked if people would miss Ascension Cares if it were suddenly discontinued, Judy replied, "Definitely, they would. People look forward to that Monday night dinner. It is the same people that come out every week. You know they would miss it."

We are sure that you would agree that this cultivation and strengthening of social ties that occurs through the community dinners is a very important antidote to social isolation and loneliness. Judy also described in considerable detail the spiritual and social benefits she experiences by volunteering with Ascension Cares:

> I am glad I got to know about this program this year. It is great to help people and to hear people's stories. One lady said, last night, that she needed pet food for her cat, and she asked [Linda for help]. She said that the bills come out all at once and [at] the end she only had thirty-six cents until Friday, which is Old Age payment day. I went home that day and thought, some days you feel so sorry for yourself. And when you listen to stories like this, you thank God and say how lucky I am . . . to be able to help these people. You feel good that you are able to help others. You take a

---

13. Donna Sousa, field notes journal, May 29, 2023.

> whole different look at your life when you can help other people. I truly enjoy it. You come away feeling good.

These comments by Judy echo our earlier discussion of another patron, Nicole, and how Ascension Cares is actively forming disciples.

Another patron, Melinda, a seventy year-old divorced woman who lives alone, stated that the fitness program offered through Ascension Cares uplifts her in a variety of ways.

> Thank God that I saw the [Ascension Cares] program last summer. So, there were interesting groups at the time, for example, the exercise [fitness] group, so I gave it a try. That is very rewarding for me. So, I joined the fitness group every Thursday morning and [Linda] is fantastic. Tom, the building overseer, is very friendly and calm. Pat, my instructor, is very knowledgeable; again, this helps [ensure] my mental, physical, social needs . . . [are] met.

We also heard from Nadia, a seventy year-old married woman who said she attends an exercise program through Ascension Cares and she used to volunteer for the community dinners. When Nadia was asked if Ascension Cares influences her perception of God and the church, she responded,

> Yes, I think it does. Like the "Cares" wraps its arms around me. Maybe it is because I am a part of . . . [Ascension] Parish that I feel I am wrapped around his love. I cannot speak to how others may feel about [Ascension Cares] when they are not a part of the parish. For me, [Ascension Cares] is a welcoming name, we care about you, come on over[,] . . . come on over and we will get together, share, and have fun.

Forming Partnerships

After these interviews we spent some more time talking with Linda, the outreach coordinator. She shared about how some local social service agencies are partnering with Ascension Cares—sometimes because they cannot house the food or clothing articles themselves:

> I was approached by [a leader from a local community agency]. . . . She wanted to talk to me about partnering with them because they refer many of their clients here for our [Help Yourself] program, our food bank, and the community meal—everything that we have. She knows that we are on grants and donations. They

do not have space for all these things so they will make financial contributions to keep our food bank stocked to help with that.

Linda's comments here about a community agency seeking a partnership with Ascension Cares reflects how the program is manifesting another aspect of the outward dimension of the flourishing congregations construct—that is, forming partnerships. Although congregations have to exercise prudence when joining forces with a community agency, so such a partnership does not compromise their Christian mission, McAlpine et al. point out that "collaborating with other organizations is an important marker of congregational flourishing" and such organizations may include those that assist persons "living with poverty, mental health concerns, and addictions."[14]

Ascension Cares *is* well-versed in this area, as it partners with local organizations such as an agency that teaches conversational English to immigrant women, a local hospice, and the local Society of St. Vincent de Paul. Furthermore, the parish website provides an application form for other agencies and organizations to partner with Ascension Cares, and the website states the team is always seeking ways to create more connections and partnerships within the community.

We think this keen interest in forming partnerships with community agencies is a unique aspect of Ascension parish. Does your congregation form partnerships with community agencies? If so, how has it been working out for you? If not, does this description of Ascension Cares prompt you to consider forming such partnerships?

CONCLUSION

At the beginning of this chapter, we invited you to compare and contrast the activities and characteristics of your congregation with Ascension parish, which includes its neighborhood involvement and evangelistic activities through Ascension Cares. What sorts of things came to your mind?

Perhaps your reflection can be even more helpful if we briefly revisit and outline our impressions of the story we were told during our case study. We noted how the Ascension Cares team demonstrated a clear sense of direction and self-identity, and we think this was bolstered by their conducting a needs assessment during the program's formative stages. By

---

14. McAlpine et al., *Signs of Life*, 187–88.

conducting a needs assessment, the team clearly envisioned specific programs they would develop to reach out to the community. This clear vision, very much linked to their strong self-identity, helped them to develop and implement neighborhood involvement efforts that are also evangelistic.

These concerted neighborhood activities involve forming partnerships with community agencies, which further accentuates the program's outward focus. Also, Ascension Cares is actively forming disciples as people experience the initiative and contribute to its growth by volunteering their time, energy, and talents. Consequently, as people's sense of discipleship grows, we think they are then even more inclined to engage in neighborhood involvement and evangelism, which, in turn, can further strengthen their sense of discipleship; this may lead to even more outreach and evangelism. Thus, Ascension parish, through Ascension Cares, has shown itself to be a flourishing congregation characterized by a synergistic process in which different aspects of flourishing, especially those pertaining to the construct's outward dimension, can interact with and reinforce each other.

We think this synergistic quality of Ascension parish, prompted by the development of the dynamic and efficacious program Ascension Cares, is most commendable. We propose that if the broader Roman Catholic Church adopted similar community outreach strategies, then more vulnerable people would be served and more people, experiencing the word of God being put into action, would respond to Jesus' call to encounter him at the Eucharistic table.

QUESTIONS FOR REFLECTION

1. What are some effective ways to conduct a needs assessment that can inform and shape a congregation's neighborhood involvement?

2. What are the best ways to create a sense of identity and direction within a congregation?

3. How can forming partnerships with community agencies be a form of evangelization?

4. What sorts of strategies can be employed to encourage patrons of church-based programs to volunteer in the same, or similar, initiatives?

BIBLIOGRAPHY

Angus Reid Institute and Cardus. "Canada across the Religious Spectrum: A Portrait of the Nation's Inter-faith Perspectives during Holy Week." Angus Reid Institute, Apr. 18, 2022. https://angusreid.org/canada-religion-interfaith-holy-week/.

Gokani, Ravi. "'Client Transformation': Spiritual and Non-spiritual Outcomes for Social Service Recipients of Evangelical Faith-Based Organisations." *Religions* 12.8.569 (2021). https://doi.org/10.3390/rel12080569.

McAlpine, Bill, et al. *Signs of Life: Catholic, Mainline, and Conservative Protestant Congregations in Canada*. Toronto: Tyndale Academic, 2021.

Statistics Canada. "Data Products, 2016 Census." Statistics Canada, last updated Feb. 8, 2021. https://www12.statcan.gc.ca/census-recensement/2016/dp-pd/index-eng.cfm.

9

Faithful Communities of Presence

Linda C. Nicholls, Sarah Han, and James Mallon

Upon learning from the diverse stories and experiences in these seven congregations, we turn now to hear from three practitioner respondents from mainline Protestant, conservative Protestant, and Catholic contexts who are well known in these denominational sectors. The purpose of this chapter is to provide broad theological, ecclesiological, and practical connections between the preceding chapters and the diverse ministry environments that you, the reader, will be located in. As you'll read, there is an invitation for church leaders and communities to be faithfully present to the Holy Spirit, to one another, and to the supporting structures and culture that undergird healthy congregational life. We begin with Anglican Archbishop Linda Nicholls.

ARCHBISHOP LINDA C. NICHOLLS, RETIRED PRIMATE, ANGLICAN CHURCH OF CANADA

As a judicatory leader I found myself cheering for each of these congregations in their approaches to congregational flourishing. There is no "one size fits all" program or set of tasks that will enable a congregation to flourish. These congregations and their leaders seized their moment in the great arc of salvation history through key commitments and values that undergird each of them. Yet each chose and found a different path to flourishing. For others seeking the same flourishing, it is encouraging to see possibilities, though it may be discouraging to some to realize that there is no simple "fix" or program to transfer to their own situation! In this reflection I want to set the learnings from these congregations alongside my own tradition (Anglican) and identify what may be helpful for others seeking that same flourishing in their faith community.

First, I want to commend the methodologies of each of the authors in using lay leaders and clergy as essential tools in assessing congregational life and in surveying their wider communities. This is especially true for new clergy who may be keen on the latest insights from their theological training yet need to take the time needed to learn their community first.

The iterative process of experiencing community events and worship; interviewing individuals and groups, including key leaders; and observations through the lens of an outsider all provide critical information in the discernment of ministry. Whether considering the life of one's own faith community or that of the community around it, it is necessary to experience its life from different vantage points. Leaders may arrive with preconceived ideas and vision. Or they may be so accustomed to "the way we do it here" that they are blinded from seeing the patterns of comfort or dis-ease and resistant to change because the ease of our patterns is hard to shift. We need the tools of observation and curiosity through experience and reflection. If unable to see one's own community differently, then visit another one—either in the same denomination or a completely different one—and observe their patterns as a reflective tool for considering your own.

I have served for over thirty years in Anglican/Roman Catholic dialogue, both in Canada and internationally. Our current method for ecumenical engagement is that of "receptive ecumenism." In this method, recognizing that an organic unity has been elusive over the past fifty years of dialogue, we examine and describe ourselves in the presence of the other. As we observe what is good and life giving in the other, we see our own shortcomings with fresh eyes and a greater willingness to change. It is not about becoming the other or being identical. Rather it is about walking in parallel as siblings in Christ so that we might learn from one another. Curiously, that brings us closer together even when continuing issues of doctrine and polity do not lend themselves to unity.

It is that practice of receiving from the other and being able to examine oneself with honesty that can arise from experiencing one's community afresh. The authors entered into the life of each congregation as an observer with a heart of curiosity to learn and receive. Lay leaders and clergy need to be able to do that in their own faith community—and equally in the wider community around them. In challenging times congregations can become defensive or shuttered to those around them, making assumptions about their needs or willingness to be engaged. It is important to listen deeply and learn from one's neighbors in order to be present as servants of Christ. Each of the authors interviewed individuals and groups, including leaders. This is a key tool for assessment, listening without judgment or bias as much as is possible, to hear what is known, felt, and experienced in order to test an approach.

The thesis of this book is the importance of stories in assisting congregations to flourish. That importance is embedded in the very DNA of being a Christian community. We know who we are by the stories we live in from the Scriptures, from our faith tradition, and from those who share the faith journey with us now. We are the people of God, followers of Jesus Christ, shaped by the salvation history stories of the Hebrew Scriptures and the Gospels: God's relationship with humankind, rooted in the life, death, and resurrection of Jesus, and developed through Acts and the epistles. In the stories of Scripture we see our own stories reflected, communal and individual, and find our way to God through them.

Our faith tradition tells the story in particular ways that become rooted in our DNA. As an Anglican, the prayers of the liturgy are formative through repetition and familiarity. The stories of the saints marked in feast days and memorials tell us how God is at work in the lives of ordinary people, like us, to reflect God's reign in amazing ways.

Every congregation has been shaped and sometimes pummelled into the community it is now by its history. The stories of previous pastors and priests; the stories of disasters overcome; the painful stories of conflict or abuse are all threads that have contributed. In addition, the behaviors of the community are embedded in systems and patterns, rooted in that history, that may need to be recognized to be understood. Some are healthy and life giving while others may be self-destructive.

The wise leaders of a community know the stories of the past and where to link the present story helpfully to those stories or begin to weave a new narrative that is healthier for this time. The skill of reframing was especially notable in chapter three in finding ways to frame the resilience of the congregation as it responded to repeated disasters.

Each of the congregations surveyed knew the importance of telling their story and ensuring that every member (or most) could tell it well. For Anglicans, this is the purpose of the liturgical year and its calendar of readings—to tell the salvation story every year in order to keep it in our hearts and minds. In particular, the liturgies of Holy Week take us into the Jesus' teachings and the drama of the conflict with human desires and sin that led to his death and to the incredible gift of the resurrection. These flourishing congregations found ways to tell their story so they are rooted in the life of every member as much as possible. They used multiple communication tools to ensure the whole community knew and could articulate their call and commitment. For some it was the creation of short statements or acknowledged values that all knew and could share. Visible posters of their commitments were posted as reminders.

As I read each chapter, I noted common threads among them that are succinctly named in chapter seven. The first thread is that of the stories of the congregation as discussed above—both descriptive (history and life now) and prescriptive (vision of who we aim to be).

A second thread is the institutional and contextual factors that each congregation recognized in and around itself. These included the historical context and current needs of the local community—immigration shifts, secularization, the need for deeper spirituality and/or community, or responding to changing issues such as LGBTQ+ conversation or poverty.

Thirdly, each needed to be adaptable and be flexible as new ideas were implemented and tried. Even when flourishing, change can be disruptive and bring conflict and strain.

Fourthly, each community engaged collaborative leadership. Each congregation engaged a variety of leaders, volunteer and staff, lay and ordained. The telling of the story and living it did not depend on the clergy or leaders alone. Lay leaders and members are fully engaged with support and training offered to connect them, build their skills, and encourage recruitment of others. Their engagement gives collective ownership to the story so it is woven deeply into the life of the community.

Lastly, they had leadership with a vision. The leaders had reflected on the needs of the congregation and community and identified a potential path forward. It would need collaborative leadership to succeed but someone needed to articulate the vision and bring it forward to be tested. It is a necessary though not sufficient requirement!

In addition, a further thread is that of context. Each congregation paid attention to the community around and within it in light of the gospel. Even though they chose different ways of responding, they were each listening to some aspect of their context that was calling them to engage. For the Catholic parish in chapter two, it was the call to the new evangelization, immigration, decline, and a new building. For the church in Quebec in chapter four, it was the urgency to meet an increasingly secular society with a message that was accessible and relevant. For the Chinese congregation of chapter six, a need to deepen spiritual formation focused their efforts.

Each chose a particular focus arising from the broader calling to make disciples, a part of our baptismal covenant with God. They might have chosen a different focus and still found a path to flourishing, as there is no single 'right' way. The primary call is to faithfulness—to listen, reflect and engage; to discern, evaluate and try again.

These parishes give us a template for that kind of faithfulness, not as a singular map but as signs that a path forward is possible in multiple ways.

REV. DR. SARAH HAN, ASSISTANT PROFESSOR OF PASTORAL MINISTRY (HOMILETICS), TYNDALE SEMINARY, DIRECTOR OF TYNDALE CENTRE FOR PASTORAL IMAGINATION

From the stories told by congregations in this book, we learn that people are the church, and congregations flourish when we engage in intentional relationships with one another and with God. As noted in chapter three, "flourishing often occurs not just in spite of, but through experiencing difficult circumstances, changes, and transitions"; individuals in these stories didn't just survive, they thrived when they were able to lean on God and battle through challenges together as a community. Healing, resilience, and joy were birthed when individuals became God's listening and loving presence to one another, reenacting Christ in the flesh through deep covenantal relationships. All the themes that enabled congregations to flourish were rooted in these kinds of flourishing relationships between individuals and with God. In each of these contexts, God uniquely revealed who he is in the relational space in between people and with himself.

Our God is a storytelling God and our relationships become the canvas upon which God paints a picture of who he is. When we share our lives with each other, God invites us to uncover the myriad layers of his nature, revealing his fearfully and wonderfully made image reflected in each of us. There is therefore something powerful about allowing another person to peer into the depths of who we are. In doing so, we become Christ to one another, inviting one another to discover the image of God that is alive within our everyday stories—both the messy and the glorious. By sharing stories and fostering deep-rooted relationships, we uncover more of God's nature through one another. It is in the liminal spaces between individuals that the beauty and intricacies of God are most profoundly revealed, leading to the flourishing of congregations.

Consistently sharing the nitty-gritty of our lives with those in our faith community therefore holds greater significance than merely getting to know one another. When we commit to sharing our joys and struggles with authenticity and vulnerability, we create more spaces for God to show up, which give us more opportunities to experience God together. As told by the stories we have read, flourishing relationships are vital to the flourishing of congregations.

The challenge I observe in Generation X, millennials, and Generation Z, is that we live in a culture of isolation, where flourishing relationships become rarer as busy rhythms of daily life don't support a communal sense of existence. One of the harmful by-products of the digital age is that online platforms have created environments for story sharing without the crucial element of face-to-face interactions rooted in intimate relationships. Many of us find ourselves isolated in silos of doom scrolling, consuming stories shared through screens without the foundation of transformative fellowship. Additionally, our digitized world has made it difficult to disconnect from work, leaving us constantly bombarded by the busyness and demands of a consumerist culture.

Several factors within ourselves can also hinder the forming of authentic and flourishing relationships with others. One common barrier is the fear of vulnerability and judgment. Many of us struggle to share openly about our hardships, burdens, and weaknesses out of fear of being judged or rejected. Additionally, busyness and distractions in life prevent us from investing the time and effort needed to build meaningful relationships of trust. The individualistic, post-secular culture we live in fosters a lack of community and a focus on self-reliance, making it challenging to truly experience God's presence in relationships. Furthermore, unresolved conflicts, misunderstandings, and lack of communication can create division and hinder the development of deep and authentic relationships within the church. Overcoming these barriers requires intentional effort, vulnerability, humility, and a commitment to prioritize the building and nurturing of covenant relationships within the body of Christ. Many of these facets are observable in the stories told by congregations in these chapters, offering valuable real-life insights on how to flourish in our relationships through persistent obedience, commitment to one another, and creative, collaborative leadership focused on God's mission.

While the stories told in this book were rooted in diverse contexts, a common theme emerged: each congregation flourished by seeing and experiencing God in their individual and communal narratives. Stories are powerful because they tap into our natural curiosity and transport us into realms of imagination filled with adventure and possibilities. Sharing of stories, therefore, becomes a powerful tool for building connections and fostering intimacy within a faith community. When we share our stories, we create communities of vulnerability and authenticity, inviting each other to discover how God is uniquely at work in our lives. As demonstrated by the congregations' stories, the very act of sharing stories can create a sense of belonging and birth shared memories, traditions, and values that allow relationships to flourish.

This is perhaps why the enemy seeks to divide the unity within the body of Christ. When our church communities are divided and relationships become fractured, it becomes increasingly difficult for God to reveal himself in our midst. However, the stories in this book demonstrate that when we connect with God and one another, miracles of resonance and resilience emerge, forming deeper community bonds as we experience God together. It is no wonder that the Bible places such an emphasis on being united as one body. When we unite in the practice of sharing our stories, we invite the powerful, flourishing presence of God into our midst, as he reveals himself in the relational spaces we create.

One of the most frequent requests my children make is, "Umma! [Mom!] Tell us a story!" They eagerly seek stories about my life, their early years, and the people we know and love. While I deeply value nurturing their curiosity and growth through storytelling, I must admit that I often find myself too fatigued, distracted, or busy to dedicate the quality time and energy needed for these moments. It makes me wonder: If I struggle to find time and energy for nurturing my own children, how will I ever make room to connect with others in flourishing relationships? In starting a church plant that aims to provide a community of faith for those longing for deeper relational connections, I've come to a humbling realization: it takes intentionality and obedience to carve out time in my day for meaningful and quality interactions with others. The stories shared by the congregations in this book remind me that consistent daily commitment to being in flourishing relationships is the most innovative and mission-focused way to lead my community.

Unfortunately, it is a common struggle that the business and busyness of leading churches often causes us to become preoccupied with administrative tasks and managerial duties, rather than placing a priority on cultivating deeper connections with our community members. It's all too easy to become ensnared in the daily grind. However, when the flourishing of relationships is compromised amidst the flurry of busywork, there is a greater propensity for burnout and leading with a lack of joy and purpose. Establishing deep and transformative friendships with God and others is paramount to the flourishing of our own lives as leaders.

As we have read these encouraging stories of how God made congregations flourish by fostering impactful relationships, it is my hope that we feel compelled and convicted to create margin in our everyday lives to share our stories and listen to the stories of others. By sharing our lives deeply and consistently, we invite God to reveal himself in surprising, personal, and transformative ways. God is waiting to be discovered within the stories held by those in our daily rhythms—our neighbors, coworkers, friends, fellow church members. We are called to take courage, make sacrifices, and carve out room for the flourishing of our everyday relationships.

Reflecting on this personally, I challenge myself: "Sarah, are you creating daily rhythms that leave room for sharing your story and listening to the stories of others? Who is God leading you into a flourishing relationship with, and how can you be a consistent and initiating presence in that person's life? What do you need to cut from your daily routine to prioritize going deeper in sharing life with those God has placed in your sphere of influence?" I hope to tackle these questions daily and reflect the obedience and resilience exemplified by those in the flourishing stories we have read. When we join God in what he is doing around us by making time to engage in others' stories, our own stories will be transformed forever.

FR. JAMES MALLON, PASTOR OF OUR LADY OF GUADALUPE PARISH, AUTHOR, AND FOUNDER OF DIVINE RENOVATION MINISTRY

Healthy things grow and bear fruit. This principle is deeply ingrained in us as human beings. It is simply how we presume the world works, and for the most part, it is what happens. If we maintain healthy soil and plant healthy seeds, those seeds will grow and, if cared for, will bear fruit. We keep our children healthy, feed them, care for them, and they grow, and eventually, bear fruit. Fruitfulness is the consequence of healthy conditions, physically, psychologically, or spiritually. Regardless of how flourishing is defined or whatever aspect of flourishing that a particular congregation or faith tradition will emphasise, any flourishing is the result of health.

St. Thomas Aquinas said, "*Gratia non tollit naturam, sed perficit.*" This can be translated as saying, "Grace does not destroy nature but perfects it."[1] This lays a solid principle of Christian anthropology that is adhered to by many Christian theological and spiritual traditions: when God is at work, human nature, including our intellect and free will is not replaced but elevated and even perfected. This means that spiritual flourishing is inextricably linked to human flourishing. For any system, organization, or community to be spiritually healthy, it must be humanly healthy.

So, congregations will flourish if they are humanly healthy. They may flourish in different ways, but the presence of fruit is unmistakable and shines forth in a landscape that is too oft characterized by a paucity of fruitfulness. At the same time, church congregations, like any other human gathering or association, will always exhibit in the collective personality the basic characteristics of the individuals who inhabit them. Human beings by instinct and impulse are biologically hardwired to seek their own personal flourishing, or the flourishing of their family, tribe, or clan, at the expense of all others. Human communities are, by default, inward-focused, self-centered and self-serving. We see these traits all too often present in many congregations who say by what they do and do not do, by what they celebrate and ignore, that they only really care about themselves and their preferences. As a result, their communities function more as clubs, set up to meet the needs and wants of their members, than as the Church of Jesus Christ, called into being to complete the work of their master, who came not to be served but to serve.

---

1. Aquinas, *Summa Theologica*, 1.1.8, ad 2.

Jorge Mario Bergoglio, during the conclave that elected him Pope Francis, wrote a few notes on a scrap of paper that he would use for his pre-conclave speech. In this speech he spoke about the sickness of the church, and how it was rooted in what he called self-referentiality. We have too often become a church "in itself, of itself and for itself." A sick church does not bear fruit and will never flourish. God does not abandon a sick church, but it will not flourish and bear much fruit.

St. Augustine once said that "without God we cannot, but without us God will not."[2] Throughout salvation history God has shown a preference to work through flawed and weak human beings. These human beings, through his grace, have been able to impact communities of various kinds and make them move in the direction of health so that they bear fruit and flourish. It is no different in our own time.

Today in much of the Western world, the Church of Christ is in a rout. Across all theological and spiritual traditions churches are experiencing decline. The former ways no longer work. The methods we deployed in a Christendom cultural context no longer bear fruit. As a result, most congregations are not only not flourishing but many are dying. In this context, we need to pay special attention to congregations that are flourishing. If we look closely at the stories told in this volume, we will find one thing in common across all the chapters. That one thing is leadership. In every example of churches that are bearing fruit is the story of the impact of a leader who was passionately committed to leading a congregation to a new way of being church. Their passion was stoked by a particular vision of how to be the church, of how to worship, how to be rooted in Christ, how to experience *koinonia*, and how to be the hands and feet of Jesus in the world. These leaders have been able to form their congregations, inspire their members to take on the task of becoming something other than they are, and to resist that temptation to make the church into a mere club for its members.

Flourishing is rooted in spiritual health. Spiritual health is intricately connected to organizational health, and healthy organizations will always have a passionate leader in the background. These leaders will resist the natural dynamic of every organization to turn inward and be self-referential and self-serving. They will seek the constant conversion of the systems that grow by intention or flounder by neglect.

Leadership, especially in the mainline Christian traditions, is a discipline that has largely been ignored in our programs of formation. It is

---

2. Augustine, *Essential Augustine*, 150.

one of the social sciences that is viewed with suspicion as it is tainted from being associated with the business world and its obsession with filthy lucre. Despite this, a close examination of the secular literature will show a preference for what many refer to as servant leadership, the very type of leadership modeled by Jesus himself. This is leadership as serving and loving, not lording over and exploiting.

As our culture moves from a post-Christian context into a pre-Christian culture, our communities will have to be intentional about sustainable leadership. This means investing in formation of pastoral leaders, supporting successful mentoring of new leaders, and being intentional about succession, especially with congregations that are flourishing in any way. Let us look briefly at each of these areas of ecclesial life.

Firstly, let us look at the formation of pastoral leaders. Our culture is now operating in a paradigm completely different than the one presumed by most of our pastoral models. This includes how we form people for ministry. The model of therapeutic pastoral care still dominates some seminaries. In this model, the primary task of the one in ministry is to care for the broken, to care for the sheep, not to be apostolic leaders who lead and mobilize their communities to advance the kingdom of God. Our churches must surely be communities in which the broken, the weak and vulnerable, are cared for, but this needs to be the responsibility of the mobilized and equipped people of God and not only of the pastoral leaders. Our seminaries need to be intentional about equipping pastoral leaders to be agents of change and transformation, to be men and women willing to take risks and innovate to find new ways forward.

As a church we need to work to establish a culture of leadership in every congregation. Every leader should be constantly on the lookout for others who have similar gifts. We need to see the normalization of mentoring and raising up others at every level of ministry in our churches and ecclesial organizations.

This leads us finally to the question of succession planning. Depending on the dominant ecclesiology, different traditions will have different practices regarding succession of leaders. Whatever our traditions around this issue, we need to embrace this responsibility with new energy and vigor. Fruitfulness or flourishing can never be taken for granted. In our present cultural context, it is the exception, and it must be protected. Every fruitful and transformed church will have had long-term leadership. However, no matter how long a leader is in place, there will come a time for that person to move on. Churches must be more intentional than ever about getting this right. The leadership needs to take great care that they recruit or appoint a new leader who is committed to the vision of that particular church and its definition of spiritual fruitfulness. They need to take great care that they are choosing a leader who will allow the spiritual garden to continue to flourish and not a leader who stifles the fruitfulness by a controlling and centralizing style.

In traditions, like my own, where pastoral leaders are appointed by the bishop, and in which the norm is a decline of the dominant ecclesial structure, the temptation can be just to find any warm body. The temptation is to manage the overall decline by slowing the decline of the entire system by a fair sharing of the pastoral wealth. Slowing the collapse of the system by a carefully managed decline only guarantees that, with time, the whole system will collapse. We need to find the courage to recognize that we are now part of a greater narrative within the Western world. As Pope Francis said, we are not in an era of change but a change of eras.[3] We are playing our part in the unfolding of the Paschal Mystery in our own time, the dying and rising of Christ lived out today in our ecclesial systems. The dying, as necessary as it is, can and should lead to life. We will not be able to save every community, but we can guarantee the continuity of the few—the few that are healthy, the few that bear fruit, the few that are flourishing, and those that flourish will provide the seeds that will be sown for the next generation of Christians in a world we are yet to imagine.

QUESTIONS FOR REFLECTION

1. What practices currently help or hinder your ability to be faithfully present to God's activity in your life and in the world?

2. What habits and postures presently impact your capacity to be faithfully present to others? What influence does your disposition have on the stories and experiences arising in your local church community?

3. Is your church intentional about creating a culture of leadership? Is recognizing, calling forth, and mentoring new leaders a part of what you do? Why or why not?

---

3. Francis, "Prato and Florence," 7–8.

4. Are the members of your church aware of how your ordained leaders are formed? What is your faith tradition doing to help form apostolic leaders?

5. Does your ecclesial culture default toward long-term leadership? If your church is flourishing, is there a plan for succession of the leader? If not, what could that look like?

BIBLIOGRAPHY

Aquinas, Thomas. *Summa Theologica.* Vol. 1. Translated by Fathers of the English Dominican Province. Westminster, MD: Christian Classics, 1981.

Augustine. *The Essential Augustine.* Edited by V. J. Bourke. New York: New American Library, 1964.

Francis. "Pastoral Visit of His Holiness Pope Francis to Prato and France." Papal address. Vatican website. Nov. 10, 2015. https://www.vatican.va/content/francesco/en/speeches/2015/november/documents/papa-francesco_20151110_firenze-convegno-chiesa-italiana.pdf.

10

Congregations That Tell Meaningful Stories

Mark Chapman, Arch Chee Keen Wong, and Joel Thiessen

STORIES ARE HOW CONGREGATIONS describe who they are. However, stories also shape congregations. They identify core values from the past and point to future expectations. Stories help to express and make meaning. Stories are important. A story rooted in the described context and experiences of a particular congregation that resonates with congregants provides the interpretive reasoning behind action, a normative framework for acting, a baseline for evaluating action, and an outline of pragmatic future action.

The stories in this book are animated by two questions: (1) What are the mechanisms, pathways, and processes that contribute to congregational flourishing? (2) How does congregational flourishing intersect with individuals, neighborhoods, and organizations? The different congregations provide answers to these questions in vastly different ways. The stories encompass broad policy and practical action. They include stories of continuity with the past and new directions. Some of the actions in these stories are driven by pastoral action and others by congregational ethos. Themes that rise to the surface to help explain congregational flourishing in the face of transition and change include the following: visionary leadership, innovative and entrepreneurial initiatives, clear congregational identity rooted in spiritual formation, intentional systems and structures oriented toward a congregation's mission and vision, hospitable community among members, and engaged laity who collectively own and participate in the congregation's mission. These themes rise out of the practical business of being the church, but in each case the congregations had developed that everyday experience into stories of how and why they did what they did and how it fit into what God was doing among them.

This theological theorizing from everyday experience can be called practical theology. John Swinton and Harriet Mowat provide this definition of practical theology:

> Practical Theology is critical, theological reflection on the practices of the Church as they interact with the practices of the world, with a view to ensuring and enabling faithful participation in God's redemptive practices in, to, and for the world.[1]

This concluding chapter uses practical theology as a framework for examining the stories in this book and how they fit together to provide resources for thinking about your own church. We first explore how these congregations came to understand what is happening in their contexts and their explanation for why it is going on. This is the raw data for how they make their stories meaningful. However, these congregations go further and explore what ought to happen in their context. The telling of meaningful stories feeds into their self-understanding and results in decisions to respond to what is going on. This response is how their stories lead them to express meaning in a practical context. This ability to identify and clearly articulate who they are and are not and how their organizational past, present, and future link together in their context is a core feature of the flourishing congregations in this book.

Richard Osmer describes that framework by discussing four core and interconnected tasks of practical theological interpretation (see also chapter five). These tasks can be implemented to guide and respond to specific episodes, situations, or contexts in ministry for pastoral leaders. They are the ways our congregations tell their stories:

- Descriptive-empirical: *What is going on?* Gathering information to better understand particular episodes, situations, or contexts.
- Interpretive: *Why is this going on?* Entering into a dialogue with the social sciences to interpret and explain why certain actions and patterns are taking place.
- Normative: *What ought to be going on?* Raising normative questions from the perspectives of theology, ethics and other fields.

1. Swinton and Mowat, *Practical Theology*, 7.

- Pragmatic: *How might we respond?* Forming an action plan and undertaking specific responses that seek to shape the episode, situation, or context in desirable directions.[2]

THE DESCRIPTIVE-EMPIRICAL AND INTERPRETIVE TASKS

We explore the first two tasks together because that is how they were experienced among many of the congregations. The descriptive-empirical task seeks to answer this question: "What is happening in each of these flourishing congregations?" The interpretive task asks: "Why are these things happening in each of these flourishing congregations?" To answer these two questions, we draw on theories—sociological, psychological, theological, and so on—to explain the multifaceted depictions of congregational practices that are described in each of the chapters by means of storytelling. Thus, practical theological interpretation takes place in a context of interdisciplinary dialogue with the social sciences.[3]

In this book you have witnessed congregations as storytelling organizations. David Boje reminds us that a storytelling organization is a "collective storytelling system in which the performance of stories is a key part of members' sense-making and a means to allow them to supplement individual memories with institutional memory."[4] In each chapter, we hope that you were able to capture the stories of *what* was happening in these seven congregations and then *why* those things occurred toward each congregation's flourishing.

In the introduction we introduced you to the Flourishing Congregations Construct: organizational ethos (self-identity, leadership, innovation, and structure and process), internal attention (discipleship, engaged laity, hospitable community, and diversity) and outward focus (neighborhood involvement, partnerships, and evangelism). This construct is woven throughout the various stories in each of the chapters. In particular, each of its domains and dimensions speak both to the context of congregational life (what is going on?) and the explanation of congregational life (why is

---

2. Osmer, *Practical Theology*, 4–12. For a concise description of Osmer's method see Osmer, "Practical Theology," 2.

3. For Osmer, interdisciplinary dialogue brings perspectives of two fields into conversation. In practical theological interpretation, this commonly is the perspective of practical theology and another field. See Osmer, *Practical Theology*, 163–72.

4. Boje, "Stories," 106.

it going on?). In the rest of this section, we use elements of the flourishing congregations construct to illustrate the stories these congregations tell of what they are doing and why they are doing it.

The organizational ethos dimensions of leadership, innovation, and structures and process construct are used by Cathy Holtmann and Sam Reimer in chapter two to tell the story of St. Jerome's as a Catholic parish that used what they called the "Game Plan" as a central strategy for equipping and keeping parishioners focused and engaged on the mission of re-evangelization and renewal. To implement this change in organizational ethos the parish leadership had to address individuals who were benefiting from the congregation but not contributing. In chapter three on St. Eustace's parish, Katie Steeves, Jason John Burtt, and Michael Wilkinson develop their concept of "repertoires of resilience" to explain the self-identity, leadership, and innovation constructs observed in the congregation. These repertoires of resilience are promulgated through shared aspirational stories, processes, and symbols that then help them face present and future uncertainties. Two challenging experiences, a fire that rendered the church building unusable and more recently COVID-19, which could have led to a deficit mindset, instead made St. Eustace's a stronger and more innovative community and built a capacity for resilience to face future challenges. The challenges reflect what was going on, but their story explained why and how they made these experiences a meaningful part of their stories as a flourishing community.

In chapter four, you will notice that we transitioned to the internal dimension: hospitable community, discipleship, diversity, and engaged laity. Frédéric Dejean uses accessibility theory to look at two conservative Protestant congregations in Quebec: La Chapelle and Axe21. Accessibility theory helps to explain why creating a culturally relevant space helps to remove barriers for some between post-Christian Quebec society and the La Chapelle and Axe21 congregations. Through hospitable community, barriers are removed to integrate newcomers. This chapter shared stories of how congregational habits need to be adjusted to make it easier for newcomers to figure out how things work in a congregation. It also illustrates how what makes sense in one context may not necessarily make sense in another context. Hospitable community was also spoken about in chapter seven. Joel Thiessen shared the story of St. Paul's Catholic Church's complicated and evolving narrative of becoming a hospitable community—a narrative of shifting from competing with other parishes for members to becoming a more authentic welcoming community. As St. Paul's frames its story around a hospitable community, it also constructs another narrative around numerical growth. This chapter shared how this parish of over four thousand parishioners before COVID-19 navigated church size and sought to create a level of interpersonal social embeddedness that would not diminish with size.

Chapters five and six also focused on the internal dimension of discipleship. This internal dimension focuses on the areas of spiritual formation and growth at both the individual and congregational level. In chapter five, Arch C. K. Wong explores the various ways in which St. John's Anglican Church told its story about spiritual formation and the means it used to encourage spiritual growth among adults, its families, and children. The social ties of connection and relationality were the "glue" that brought together this congregation's way of discipleship. Spiritual formation happened in relationships and knowing the other. Dr. Sarah Han's practitioner response in the last chapter further reinforces the significance of relationship with one another and with God. In addition, Mark Chapman, Andrea Chang, and James Watson in chapter six looked at a Chinese church's founding vision (Still Waters) and its supportive spiritual disciplines. These have shaped the development of the congregation and the lives of its members into a particular story of congregational flourishing. They use Hartmut Rosa's resonance theory to explore relationship with God and with one another in community. The spiritual disciplines are a way of responding to God's call on their lives. In this response the congregation is changed. A notable aspect of their story is the understanding that there is an element of uncontrollability and mystery to this process. This reminds us that even when congregations know their context well and have some sense of why things are going on, outcomes are not guaranteed. The stories of the congregations are always developing and changing.

Chapter eight by Bernardine Ketelaars and Fr. Robert Weaver tells the story of Ascension Church's parish-based community outreach program. This speaks to the outward dimension of the construct (neighborhood involvement, partnerships, and evangelism) and helps us articulate the various ways that Ascension Church, including its congregants, are involved in initiatives beyond the walls of the parish. These include assisting individuals and families in need in the parish and the local community and encouraging the formation of intentional disciples of Jesus Christ in the process.

In these stories we see how the descriptive-empirical task and, in particular, the interpretive task help us see how theology and the social sciences come together to improve our understanding of what these congregations are doing and why they are doing it. These diverse stories illustrate different ways that congregations can flourish. Such interdisciplinary dialogue draws on both the empirical tools of the social sciences and on the normative tools provided by theology to which we now turn.

THE NORMATIVE TASK

In the previous section we engaged extensively with the Flourishing Congregations Construct because the construct focuses on the descriptive and to so some degree the interpretive tasks. While the construct remains relevant in the normative and pragmatic tasks, each chapter primarily takes place in a particular context with particular people. The stories are more about the specific ways that individual congregations are flourishing rather than the general features of flourishing churches.

The normative task seeks to answer the question: "What should be happening in this situation?" Osmer suggests three approaches to the normative task:

> The first is a style of theological reflection that I call here theological interpretation: the use of theological concepts to interpret episodes, situations, and contexts, including those in which we are the actors. . . . A second way of approaching this episode normatively [is] the use of ethical norms to reflect on and guide practice. . . . A third approach [is] offering examples of good practice.[5]

Although not mutually exclusive, these three approaches are interpretive guides in carrying out the normative task. Most of the chapters in this book take up the normative task by using the good practice and/or theological interpretation approaches. These congregational stories are examples of ways that pastoral leaders could approach theological reflection on aspects of congregational flourishing. Theology tells us what ought to be in a particular congregation. The social sciences provide tools to describe what is empirically present in a congregation. Part of what we are trying to accomplish in this book is to encourage practitioners to embrace these different ways of knowing as they serve the purposes of the church. We have intentionally

---

5. Osmer, *Practical Theology*, 131–32.

chosen authors that straddle the line between the two disciplines and have included three responses by practitioners to root the conversation in the work of the church. Thus, when we talk of interdisciplinary dialogue[6] we are talking about how the social sciences provide a rich description of congregational contexts and empirical theories for practical theologians and pastoral leaders that make for a fulsome and comprehensive picture for the field of theology to consider in its theological reflections and in pastoral/congregational action. Likewise, the work of theology helps the social scientist studying congregations to know what to explore and helps explain why it should be explored. For example, each of the practitioner responses explore practices that are currently shaping the contemporary church and how we can look to our theological norms for guidance in adjusting to new circumstances.

These responses are their reflections on the several examples of interdisciplinary conversations in the various chapters, examples that examine ways that the normative task can be approached. For example, Steeves, Burtt, and Wilkinson (chapter 3) describe "repertoires of resilience" as a way of framing challenging moments in the history of a congregation that may lead to future possibilities of flourishing. Pastoral leaders may enter into conversations with the concept of "repertoires of resilience" as St. Eustace's did around the charred cross from the old parish that hung in a prominent place in the new building. The normative task of theological interpretation sees the cross as a place of suffering and hope and strength. A theology of the cross seeks to hold the divine and human action together and asks what the continuing ministry of Jesus in the world looks like. To put it another way, the continuing ministry of Jesus affects pastoral action in the world and the church. The charred cross speaks to the lived experience and informs the concrete way that the priest uses to speak to and teach the congregation such that they can grow and become stronger from the fire as opposed to disheartened.

Theological norms and social science also come together in the discussion of hospitality. Dejean (chapter 4) uses accessibility theory to explain how the congregation welcomed others outside of the congregational walls into the life of the church community in a way that reflects a language of welcome for a broader Quebecois society. Thiessen (chapter 7) examines hospitality more from an internal perspective but also utilizes social embeddedness theory to address how numerical growth was incorporated

---

6. See Osmer, *Practical Theology*, 159–72.

into this congregation's story. These two studies show how pastoral leaders could engage the Christian tradition of hospitality as a moral imperative to welcome strangers or guests and treat them justly. From a theological perspective, it sees strangers or guests as made in the image of God. In terms of carrying out the normative task, this approach to good practice for pastoral leaders can be informed by a sociological understanding of the context. Such stories could inform how others could welcome religious nones, strangers, and guests in all their diversity.

A final example of interdisciplinary conversation between theology and the social sciences comes from Chapman, Chang, and Watson's use of resonant relationships (chapter 6) to help illuminate theological experience and Wong's utilization of social network analysis (chapter 5) as it applies to discipleship and spiritual formation. Pastoral leaders can come to understand how discipleship and spiritual formation contribute to the normative task from observing good practices of other congregations. Furthermore, how these congregations explain their practice can be a foundation for figuring out what this practice should look like in other contexts. Osmer explains that good practice provides normative guidance in two ways: (1) It offers a model of good practice from the past or present with which to reform a congregation's present actions. (2) It can generate new understandings of God, the Christian life, and social values beyond those provided by the received tradition.[7]

Models of good practices around discipleship and spiritual formation provide pastoral leaders and congregations assistance in innovating and imagining how spiritual growth may be done differently or better in order to lead to flourishing. The observations from the researchers of Still Waters and St. John's Anglican Church are two models of good practice around discipleship and spiritual formation that pastoral leaders may learn from.

We now shift our attention to the pragmatic task and address the pragmatic question of how action should be taken.

PRAGMATIC TASK

The pragmatic task says that given that we have figured out, to the best of our ability, what is going on, why it is going on, and have followed our theology of what should be going on, how then do we respond? The work of flourishing congregations is not simply descriptive and theoretical.

7. Osmer, *Practical Theology*, 152.

CONGREGATIONS THAT TELL MEANINGFUL STORIES

Flourishing congregations are going about the business of being the church and following God's call on their lives. This means that they take concrete actions toward their end goal (telos). Even when the congregations in this volume were not moving quickly, they were nevertheless in motion. None of them claimed to have arrived. The stories they told were of next steps and new opportunities. To explore the pragmatic task of responding to what God is doing around them, we will examine how these congregations tell stories, the nature of their leadership, the role of their congregations, briefly touch on their physical space, and then summarize what this all means in terms of implementation.

The congregations in this volume tell stories that create worlds that shape how people engage one another and their congregations as a whole. These stories are both descriptive of where they have been and predictive of where they are going in the sense that they shape how these congregations move into the future. For example, "repertoires of resilience" both explain how a congregation has thrived despite past difficulties and gives confidence that a congregation can travel fruitfully through the difficulties of the future. The history of these congregations were not without difficult circumstances, but the challenges and transitions they encountered led to innovation and resilience. This is in part a function of the stories they have told and the stories they have lived.[8] The first response is to tell stories of resilience. Archbishop Linda Nicholls reiterates in a different way how each congregation is shaped by its history in the stories it tells about its pastoral leadership, the stories of challenges overcome, and so forth.

The second area of storytelling that we will highlight is the role of leadership. In many of the stories of these congregations, storytelling played a pivotal role in defining and defending clear self-identity and in providing clear and consistent congregational communication. Fr. James Mallon's practitioner response reinforces the importance of leadership and the ways that congregations need to build a culture of leadership and tell the story of that culture through, for example, mentoring. In chapter two we saw that St. Jerome's, in the face of declining numbers of Catholics, decades of controversy, and rising immigration, were appointed a visionary leader by their bishop, a leader who helped them tell a new story about themselves. The result was a high level of lay involvement and strong commitment to their vision of becoming "explosively alive."

---

8. Watts, *Spiritual Turn*, 153.

The story of St. Jerome's points to another pragmatic response that threads itself through these stories: the active involvement of congregants as partners in the ministry versus being a passive audience. This is most overt in chapters 5 and 6, which tell the stories of congregations whose primary focus is spiritual formation. In both cases, the story that brought these communities together for common purposes was a primary focus on a deepening of intimate relationships with God. Yet, despite this common purpose the stories they told were quite different. At St. John's the path to spiritual formation traveled through the well-known structures of the liturgy, preaching, Bible study, and family ministry. St. John's illustrates that congregational involvement that contributes to flourishing does not need radical change. Rather it can be an intentional emphasis on effective use of the familiar practices of the church. The story of congregational involvement at Still Waters includes some of the same practices as St. John's but also draws heavily on spiritual disciplines such as *lectio divina* and spiritual direction, which are less common in conservative Protestant churches. The key point for application is that there are a wide range of ways to engage congregants actively in the life and purposes of the church. As we saw in the previous paragraph, a good leader draws from the resources of the congregation and the tradition to tell the story of why and how congregants should be involved.

The pragmatic task of congregations is facilitated by effective leadership and congregational involvement, but it is also facilitated by physical space and the stories congregations tell about that space. We encountered stories of how space contributed to flourishing in St. Jerome's new building and St. Eustace's use of the burnt cross from their previous church building. However, this theme comes across particularly strong in chapter 4 where we read of the stories of two churches that have chosen to hold their services in theater spaces to make them more accessible in their post-Christian Quebec context. Such "religious safe spaces" remove unnecessary impediments to church involvement. La Chapelle take this attention to the church experience to the level of being aware that people in that context are reportedly more comfortable with a coffee in their hands and that the coffee in their hands should be good coffee. St. Paul's (chapter 7) is a contrasting example of the role of physical space. This congregation is an amalgamation of two other congregations that realized that thriving required developing a new identity for the combined congregation and that a new physical space could contribute to that storyline. A third storyline would be the Ascension Cares program in chapter 8, which describes how a congregation has leveraged its space to feed and provide a social space for their neighbors. Each of these congregations has followed their own storyline to use physical space in a way that contributes to congregational flourishing. Here again, we see that flourishing is not a function of a particular action as much as choosing and engaging in that action in a way that aligns with how God has already gifted the congregation.

There are other examples of how these flourishing congregations have engaged in the pragmatic task. However, these few themes illustrate how these congregations are flourishing, identify that there are many ways to flourish, and highlight how these congregations are implementing flourishing. Flourishing churches don't just tell stories, they leverage those stories to move into the future and this involves attention to organizational ethos. They know who they are, they have effective leadership, they innovate in line with their history and context, and they shape their structures and process to facilitate what God has called them to accomplish. Organizational effectiveness sets them up for both internal and external action. Internally an engaged laity is a fundamental factor in flourishing. Engaged laity are equipped for involvement through discipleship and hospitable community in a context that embraces diversity in the congregation. The organizational and inward stories facilitate the outward story as congregations develop partnerships, get involved in their neighborhoods, and evangelize. In all cases these congregations are leveraging a social science description of their context and responding to what is going on around them. Their theology provides the norms for action that lead to a pragmatic response. They are acting but in the knowledge that their normative and cultural context points in a particular direction. That is, theology and social science come together to provide support for discerning the story of the congregation.

SUMMARY

Stories are the currency of congregational flourishing. Congregations are storytelling organizations and how they tell those stories matters. Stories help congregations identify what is and envision what could be. Stories are embodied in people and in congregations. Who tells the story and how they tell the story shapes how it is received and the way in which it comes to be embedded in the congregational ethos. Once part of the organizational ethos, stories become performances that help people maintain the vision of what God has called them to and how they can travel that journey together.

Stories establish the narratives and set the backdrop for how the life of the congregation is lived out. Stories tell how congregations understand their leaders, how they engage their physical spaces, and why certain actions are chosen over others. Stories make congregational involvement meaningful.

A meaningful story is one that makes choices about what to prioritize, what to include, and what to leave out. It helps the congregation identify what is going on, why it is going on, what should be going on, and how to respond to it. A strong story facilitates adaptation to the inevitable changes and threats that they will confront. Do they tell a story of hardship, loss, and suffering that immobilizes them and turns them inward in a stance of trying to protect and control what they already have? Or do they take those same difficult circumstances and tell a story of adaptation and resilience as they have found God sufficient for whatever they have encountered? If they choose the second path, they are more likely to embrace adaptive change and leverage it for external engagement and renewal.

A meaningful story of adaptation and resilience is collectively owned and contributes to collective agency. None of the stories told in this volume are stories of individuals. While effective leadership played an important role, in all cases the stories were shared stories. These congregations knew who they were and because of that could move together to embrace whatever circumstance they encountered. Different congregations, different stories, but all flourishing because they worked with rather than against what God was already doing in and among them. This is the story of this book. What is God already doing in your congregation and what is he calling you to? What is your story?

BIBLIOGRAPHY

Boje, David M. *Storytelling Organizations*. Thousand Oaks, CA: SAGE, 2008.
Osmer, Richard R. *Practical Theology: An Introduction*. Grand Rapids: Eerdmans, 2008.
———. "Practical Theology: A Current International Perspective." *HTS Theological Studies* 67 (2011) 1–7. https://hts.org.za/index.php/hts/article/view/1058/2098.
Swinton, John. *Practical Theology and Qualitative Research Methods*. London: SCM Press, 2006.
Watts, Galen. *The Spiritual Turn: The Religion of the Heart and the Making of Romantic Liberal Modernity*. Oxford: Oxford University Press, 2022.

Index

accessibility theory, 44, 48–55, 138. *See also* hospitable community
Alpha Canada, 16–17
amalgamation of parishes
    St. Eustace's Anglican parish, 33, 37
    St. Jerome's Catholic parish, 12–14, 25–26
    St. Paul's Catholic parish, 95, 98–100
Ammerman, Nancy, 4
Anglican faith, 68, 124, 125. *See also* Nicholls, Linda; St. Eustace's Anglican parish; St. John's Anglican Church
Angus Reid Survey, 110
Appreciative Inquiry event
    data collection from, 7
    St. John's Anglican Church, 65, 75
    St. Paul's Catholic Parish, 94
Aquinas, Saint, 130
Ascension Cares program
    Bountiful Basket service, 116–17
    discipleship formed through, 120
    forming partnerships through, 118–19
    growth and formation through, 114–16
    inception of, 110–11
    interviews of Ascension Cares patrons, 117–18
    needs assessment for, 111
    as service-oriented evangelism, 112–14

Ascension Church
    Ascension Cares program inception, 110–11
    Bountiful Basket program, 113, 116–17
    community dinners, 115, 117–18
    demographics of, 109–10
    discipleship, 120
    Evangelism, 108–9, 112, 120
    growth and formation through, 114–16
    Help Yourself program, 113, 116, 118
    leadership of, 110–11
    neighborhood involvement of, 108–10, 112, 119–20, 139
    partnerships of, 118–20
    self-identity of, 111, 119–20
aspirational capital, 32
aspirational narratives and stories, 32, 34–36, 41, 70–72
Augustine, Saint, 131
Axe21
    accessibility theory and, 44, 48–55, 138
    COVID-19 pandemic effects on, 55–56
    hospitable community and, 138–39
    methodology of study of, 43–44
    relevance of to secular Quebec, 55–57
    religious entrepreneurship and, 45–48
    religious metalanguage example from, 50–52

INDEX

Axe21 (continued)
　as religious safe space, 52–53
　ritual removal and, 54–55
　self-identity of, 47, 61

Baptist faith, 45, 49–50
Barthes, Roland, 49
Bedard, Bob, 12
Berger, Peter, 47
Bible study groups, 68–69, 74, 80, 82
Boje, David, 1–2, 7, 137
Bountiful Basket program, 113, 116–17
Burtt, Jason John, 138
business opportunities, identifying, 46

Calhoun, Adele Ahlberg, 80
"called out to act," 84–85, 86
Canadian Conference of Catholic Bishops (CCCB), 15
Canadian Evangelical faith-based organizations (FBOs) clients, 113–14
Catholic faith. *See also* Ascension Church; Mallon, James; St. Jerome's Catholic Parish; St. Paul's Catholic Parish
　decline in congregant numbers of, 12–13, 43, 110
　priest shortage in Canada of, 20
　vs. Protestantism, 99, 104
　in Quebec, 44–45
　sexual abuse crimes in, 13
Catholicism, Roman. *See* Ascension Church
Center Church (Keller), 56–57
Chang, Andrea, 139
Chapman, Mark, 139
children, 22–23, 69–72, 75–76
churches
　adapting to secularism, 44, 84, 125
　concept of, 35–36
　contemporary operation of, 84–85
　culture and identity of, 3–5
　demographic considerations and, 71–72
　growth of, 96–98
　innovation of, 21–22
　leadership impacting, 25–27, 104, 131–33
　in modern Quebec, 43–44, 55
　perception of, 118
　relevant, 55–61
　resonance and life of, 89–91
　revitalizing, 16
　sense of belonging to, 16–17
　sickness of, 131
　social programs of, 113–14
　spiritual disciplines and, 87
collaborative leadership, 40–41, 125
collective ownership, 8, 100–101, 103–4
communities
　barriers to building, 127–29
　LGBTQ2+, 33, 34–35, 37–38
　openness to other churches and, 123–24
　racialized, 32
　self-centered nature of human, 130–31
community service, 59–60
community trust and ownership, 40
conditions of belief, religious, 47–48
congregations
　culture and identity of, 3–5
　flourishing, 5–6
　identity of, 4–5
　methodology of study of, 7–9, 11–12
　pragmatic tasks of, 143, 144–45
　size of, 6, 11
　as storytelling organizations, 1–3
　strain on, 97, 99, 103
contemplative worship, 80–83
correlational dialog, 64–65
COVID-19 pandemic impacts
　on Ascension Church, 112
　on Axe21, 55–56
　on La Chapelle, 45–46
　on St. Eustace's Anglican parish, 31, 33–34, 38
　on St. Jerome's Catholic Parish, 17, 21–22
　on St. John's Anglican Church, 63–64, 68–70
　on St. Paul's Catholic Parish, 95–97, 103

148

INDEX

cross-disciplinary dialogue, 64–65
Csordas, Thomas, 49
culture
    aspirational capital and, 32
    church, 3–4
    church compatible with modern, 48–55
    congregational, 3–4
    of congregational volunteerism, 23–24
    Evangelist, 48–49
    interparish relations and, 99–100
    Keller's four models of how evangelicals relate to, 56–57
    post-Christian context of, 132
    of Quebec, 47
    secular, 44, 47–48, 57, 59, 84, 125, 127–28, 132

deficit mindset, 138
Dejean, Frédéric, 138, 141
demographics, 4, 7, 71–72, 102–3, 109–10
descriptive-empirical tasks, 64, 136, 137–40
diocesan rule of baptism, 115
discipleship
    Ascension Church and, 116, 120
    contemplative worship approach to, 82–83
    defined, 66
    formed though Ascencion Cares participation, 116, 120
    generational diversity connected to, 70
    good models of, 142
    from religious social networks, 72–74
    spiritual formation and growth and, 139
    St. Jerome's Catholic Parish and, 12, 24–25, 27
    St. John's Anglican Church and, 65–66, 70, 72–74
diversity, 49, 69–72, 79–80, 142, 145

ecumenism, receptive, 123–24
Evangelism. *See also* Ascension Church; Axe21; La Chapelle
    Catholic aim of, 109
    Keller's four models for relating to culture by, 56–57
    offensive to secular society, 59
    in Quebec, 44–45
    sheltered enclave theory and, 48–49
    Still Waters church, 88–89

families, 69–72, 75–76, 99
"fatigue d'être eglise," 84
flourishing. *See also* relevant churches; repertoires of resilience
    barriers to, 127–29, 130–31
    clarity of identity and, 102
    community service contributing to, 59–60
    as fluid and dynamic concept, 99
    function of stories in, 63
    markers of in theology, 5–6
    "re-flourishing," 33–34
    relationships central to, 126–27
    repertoires of resilience and, 31–32
    resonant relationships and, 79
    spiritual, 130
    visionary leadership contributing to, 19–20
Flourishing Congregations Construct, 5, 88, 138–40. *See also* entries for individual dimensions
Francis (pope), 131, 133
"free riders," 23

God, 56–57, 69, 84, 124, 126–29.
Gokani, Ravi, 113–14
grace, 86–87, 115, 130, 131
growth mindset, 96–98

Han, Sarah, 9, 126–29, 139
Hatch, Nathan, 49–50
Help Yourself program, 113, 116, 118
homilies, 12, 19, 35, 68
Hopewell, James, 2, 63, 102
hospitable community, 44, 54, 98–104, 138–39, 145
hospitality
    examination of, 141–42
    inside and outside of the church, 88

INDEX

hospitality (continued)
    in St. Jerome's Catholic Parish, 16–17, 18, 19
    in St. John's Anglican church, 70, 72
    in Still Waters church, 83
Hunter, James Davison, 56, 57

identity, 4–5. *See also* self-identity
immigrants, 14, 45, 59–60
inclusivity, 30, 34–35, 37–38, 52–53, 57–58
Indigenous residential schools, 58–59
innovation, 5–6, 14, 21–22, 34–36, 46
intentional leadership, 131. *See also* St. Paul's Catholic Parish
internal dimension of flourishing congregations construct. *See also* entries for individual dimensions
    discipleship, 5–6, 12, 24–25, 27, 65–66, 70, 72–74, 82–83, 120, 139, 142
    diversity, 5–6, 49, 68–72, 142, 145
    engaged laity, 5–6, 20–21, 74, 135–36, 145
    hospitable community, 5–6, 44, 54, 98–104, 138–39, 145
interpretive tasks, 64, 136, 137–40
isolation, 117, 127

J'aime ma ville program, 59–60
Jesus Christ
    discipleship and, 24–25
    leadership inspired by, 131–32
    neighborhood involvement central to, 108–9, 113–15
    New Evangelization and, 15–16
    Still Waters church's vision and, 79

Keller, Timothy, 56–57
Keller's four models of Evangelicals relating to culture, 56–57
Ketelaars, Bernardine, 139

La Chapelle
    accessibility theory and, 44, 48–55, 138
    diversity and, 49

evangelism and, 59
hospitable community and, 138
J'aime ma ville program of, 59–60
methodology of study of, 43–44
relevance of to secular Quebec, 56–60
religious entrepreneurship and, 45–48
as religious safe space, 52–53
ritual removal and, 54–55
self-identity of, 61
laity, engaged, 11, 20–21, 74, 135–36, 145
leader intentionality, 39–40
leadership
    Ascension Church, 110–11
    changes in, 100–101
    collaborative, 40–41, 125
    flourishing congregations and, 125
    formation of, 132–33
    importance of for congregational flourishing, 131–32
    intentional, 131
    limitations of, 105
    role of storytelling to, 143
    in St. Eustace's Anglican parish, 39–41
    in St. Jerome's Catholic Parish, 12, 19–21, 25–26
    in St. John's Anglican Church, 75
    in St. Paul's Catholic Parish, 96, 100–101, 104–5
lectio divina, 79, 81
LGBTQ2+ communities, 33, 34–35, 37–38
liberal Romanticism, 50
liturgy, 18–19, 22, 67, 74, 124–25. *See also* music
Lougheed, Richard, 44–45
love, 57, 67, 69, 79, 113

Mallon, James, 9, 130–33, 143
Marti, Gerardo, 20
McAlpine, Bill, 119
McMullin, Steve, 71
Messy Church program, 70–71
Methodist tradition, 49–50

150

INDEX

"moved" characteristic of resonant relationships, 86
music, 18, 20–21, 54, 67, 71–72

neighborhood involvement, 5–6, 83, 108–10, 112, 119–20
New Evangelization, 15–16
Nicholls, Linda, 9, 122–26, 143
non-Christians, 51, 56, 113–14
normative tasks, 64–65, 136, 140–42

organizational ethos dimension of flourishing congregations construct. *See also* entries for individual dimensions
    innovation, 5–6, 14, 21–22, 34–36, 46, 138
    leadership, 5–6, 12, 18–23, 25–26, 39–41, 75, 100–101, 104–5, 110–11, 125, 131–33, 138, 143
    self-identity, 5–6, 47, 61, 79, 83, 90, 111, 119–20, 143
    structure and process, 5–6, 22–27, 79–83, 88–90, 138
Osmer, Richard, 64–65, 136, 140, 142
outward dimension of flourishing congregations construct. *See also* entries for individual dimensions
    Evangelism, 5–6, 44–45, 48–49, 56–57, 59, 88–89, 108–9, 112, 120
    neighborhood involvement, 5–6, 83, 108–9, 112, 119–20
    partnerships, 5–6, 59, 88–89, 94–95, 98, 118–20

partnerships, 88–89, 94–95, 98, 118–20
Paschal Mystery, 133
Pitt, Richard N., 46
"Pleasure of Text, The" (Barthes), 49
portable practices, 54
post-Christian culture, 43
practical theology
    descriptive-empirical tasks, 64, 136, 137–40
    interpretive tasks, 64, 136, 137–40
    normative tasks, 64, 136, 140–42
    pragmatic tasks, 64, 136, 142–45
preaching, 18–19
Protestant faith, 5, 43–45, 99, 104.

Quiet Revolution, 44

"re-flourishing," 33–34
Reimer, Sam, 4, 138
relevance, defined, 56
relevant churches, 55–60
religious entrepreneurship, 43, 45–48. *See also* Axe21; La Chapelle
religious institutional entrepreneurs, 19–21, 22–27
religious metalanguage, 50–52
religious social networks, 72–74
renewal, 16–17, 33–35. *See also* St. Jerome's Catholic Parish
repertoires of resilience, 31–41, 44, 138, 141, 143
Re-pitching the Tent (Giles), 35
resilience, 103
resonance, 83–85, 88–91
resonant relationships
    defined, 78, 85
    "moved" characteristic of, 86
    "response" characteristic of, 86–87
    "transformed" characteristic of, 87–88
    "uncontrollability" characteristic of, 88–89
"response" characteristic of resonant relationships, 86–87
rituality, removing, 54–55
Root, Andrew, 86
Rosa, Harmut, 83–84

safe spaces, religious, 52–53
secularism
    church adaptation to, 44, 84, 125
    church locations and, 4
    conditions of belief and, 47–48
    evangelism offensive to audience of, 59
    fostering lack of community, 127–28
    relevants and, 57
    service and, 132

INDEX

self-centeredness, 130–31
self-identity
    clarity of, 61, 101–2, 111, 119–20, 143
    congregational vision and, 90
    contemplative worship approach and, 79
    healthy and not-so-healthy aspects to, 47
    musical liturgy and, 67
    resilience and, 35–36
    spiritual disciplines and, 83
service-oriented evangelization, 112–16
sheltered enclave theory, 48–50
Smith, James K. A., 84
social embeddedness theory, 141–42
social science, 2–3, 64–65, 131–32, 137, 140
social scientists, 3
social ties, 72–76, 117–18. *See also* religious social networks; resonance
Somers, Margaret, 32
SongSelect (Christian Copyright Licensing International (CCLI)), 18
Sousa, Donna, 116–17
spiritual direction ministry, 82–83, 87
spiritual disciplines, 87, 139
spiritual formation and growth
    contemplative worship approach to, 80–83, 139
    defined, 66
    excellent preaching important to, 68
    generational diversity contributing to, 69–72
    role of liturgy in, 67
    small group study context supporting, 68–69
    social networks contributing to, 72–74
    Still Waters church organized around, 90
spiritual health, 87, 131
St. Eustace's Anglican parish
    amalgamation of, 33, 37
    community trust and ownership in, 40

    COVID-19 pandemic effects on, 31, 33–34, 38
    history of, 33–34
    inclusivity and, 30, 34–35, 37–38
    innovation and, 34–36
    leadership of, 39–41
    methodology of study of, 3
    repertoires of resilience and, 138
    resilience of, 33–41
    self-identity of, 35–36
    stories, culture, and resilience of, 31–32
St. Jerome's Catholic Parish
    Alpha course, 16–17
    amalgamation of, 13–14, 25–26
    Appreciative Inquiry event, 11, 12, 24
    Companions of the Cross, 12
    COVID-19 pandemic effects on, 17, 21
    culture of, 23–24
    discipleship in, 12, 24–25, 27
    engaged laity of, 11, 20–21
    Formed, video subscription used by, 17
    Game Plan of, 12, 25, 27, 138
    historical context of decline in numbers of, 12–14
    hospitality of, 16–17, 18, 19
    innovation in, 21–22
    innovation of, 14, 21
    leadership in, 12, 18–23, 25–26
    life groups and, 17
    liturgy of, 18–19, 22
    methodology of study of, 11–12
    New Evangelization of, 15–16
    self-identity of, 15–16
    structure and process in, 22–27
    Sunday Mass of, 18–19
St. John's Anglican church
    Appreciative Inquiry event, 65, 75
    Bible study groups and, 68–69
    discipleship in, 70, 72–74
    engaged laity of, 74
    generational diversity in, 69–72
    hospitality of, 70, 72
    liturgy of, 67, 74
    Messy Church program, 70–71

methodology of study of, 65
philosophy on spiritual formation, 64, 139
qualities of contributing to growth and spiritual formation, 67–69
self-identity of, 67
social ties and networking in, 72–76
spiritual formation and growth in, 64, 67–74
St. Paul's Catholic Parish
    amalgamation of, 95, 98–100
    Appreciative Inquiry event, 94
    collective ownership and, 100–1, 103–4
    commonality with other congregations, 101–5
    COVID-19 pandemic effects on, 95–96
    growth mindset of, 96–98
    hospitable community and, 98–104, 139
    leadership in, 96, 100–101, 104–5
    methodology of study of, 93–94
    partnerships of, 94–95, 98
    resilience of, 103
    self-identity of, 101–2
    transitions of, 94–96
Stark, Rodney, 72–73
Steeves, Katie, 138
Still Waters church
    contemplative worship approach to, 80–83
    discipleship in, 82–83
    diversity and, 79–80
    hospitality of, 83, 88
    neighborhood involvement of, 83
    resonance in, 83–85
    resonant relationships and, 85–89
    self-identity of, 79, 83, 90
    spiritual disciplines and, 87
    spiritual formation and growth in, 80–83, 90
    story of, 79–83
    structure and process in, 79–83, 88, 90
    Taizé services offered by, 80–81

    vision of, 78, 79, 90
stories, 63, 102–3, 128–29, 135
storytelling, 143, 145–46
storytelling organizations, 1–9, 137, 145–46
structure and process, 5–6, 22–27, 79–83, 88, 90
succession planning, 132–33
Sutcliffe, Kathleen M., 103
Swidler, Ann, 32

Taizé services, 80–81
Taylor, Charles, 47–48
theological interpretation, 140
theology, flourishing markers in, 5–6
theology, practical. *See* practical theology
Thiessen, Joel, 138–39, 141–42
thoughtful preaching, 135
traditions, changing, 23
transformational dialog, 64–65
"transformed" characteristic of resonant relationships, 87–88
transversal dialog, 64–65
trust, 13, 20, 23, 40, 68–69

"uncontrollability" characteristic of resonant relationships, 88–89

Vogus, Timothy J., 103
volunteers
    Ascension Cares and, 115–20
    collective ownership and, 100–101
    J'aime ma ville and, 59–60
    lay leadership and, 21–24
    pandemic affecting, 95

Watson, James, 139
Watts, Galen, 7, 50, 101
Weaver, Robert, 139
wholistic Christian spirituality, 81
Wilkinson, Michael, 4, 138
Wong, Arch Chee Keen, 139, 142

youth, 22–23, 50–51, 69–72, 75–76